Fave con la Buccia
WHOLE FAVA

Cicerchie
CICERCHIE

Lenticchie
LENTIL

Cannellini
CANNELLINI

Fagioli di Lamon
FAGIOLI DI LAMON

FAGIOLI

JUDITH BARRETT

coauthor of RISOTTO *and author of* SAVED BY SOUP

FAGIOLI

The Bean Cuisine of Italy

RODALE

Printed in Canada
Rodale Inc. makes every effort to use acid-free ∞, recycled paper ♻.
Photographs by Mitch Mandel/Rodale Images
Book design by Tara Long

Library of Congress Cataloging-in-Publication Data

    Barrett, Judith, date.
        Fagioli : the bean cuisine of Italy / Judith Barrett.
            p.   cm.
      Includes index.
      ISBN 1–57954–724–9 hardcover
      1. Cookery (Beans)   2. Beans—Italy.   3. Cookery, Italian.   I. Title.
    TX803.B4B37   2004
    641.6'565'0945—dc22   2004011270

Distributed to the trade by Holtzbrinck Publishers

2   4   6   8   10   9   7   5   3   hardcover

RODALE

WE **INSPIRE** AND **ENABLE** PEOPLE TO IMPROVE
THEIR LIVES AND THE WORLD AROUND THEM

FOR **MORE** OF OUR **PRODUCTS**
WWW.RODALESTORE.COM
(800) 848-4735

FOR DAVID

CONTENTS

ACKNOWLEDGMENTS

My research for this book took me all over Italy. Both old friends and acquaintances and many people I did not know before shared their knowledge, their cooking techniques, their food, and their homes with me. With their considerable help, I was able to pursue the bean trail from Lecce to Bra, from Naples to Udine, and from San Remo to Ancona. And I was as surprised and delighted by the regional diversity of bean dishes that still exists in Italy today as I was refreshed by the overwhelming generosity I encountered everywhere I went.

In Italy, I owe special thanks to those who guided, fed, and informed me: Bean growers Mario Agostinelli in Regello and Enzo Pistelli and his family in Terni showed me bean cultivation firsthand; Lori DeMori in Florence shared her intimate knowledge of the local cuisine; restaurateurs Rino and Guia Krcivoj in Tricesimo, Romano Tamani in Quistello, Matteo and Christina Ascheri in Bra, Paolo and Barbara Massieri in San Remo, and Rino and Lucia Botte in Barile all prepared special regional bean dishes for me and shared their recipes; Francesco and Giovanella Giavazzi provided me with sources and stories; Alberto and Susan Alesina rescued vital source material for me; Baronessa Cecelia Bellelli Baratta in Capaccio graciously shared her home and recipes; Rosella Speranza arranged an engaging and enlightening tour of Puglia; Bianca Tragni in Altamura added insight into the culinary history of Puglia; Domenico Maggi interpreted the contemporary culinary practices of Puglia; Costanza La Grua in Lecce opened her kitchen and shared her table with me; Simona Cardone in Bari was an eloquent and tireless translator; and Iris Carulli introduced me to the food markets of Rome.

Closer to home, I am first and foremost indebted to my friends, Ann Berman and Sam Spektor, for their generosity and hospitality, and for eagerly sharing their knowledge and enthusiasm for the cuisine of Italy with me. Arthur Schwartz generously included me in his cooking school's itinerary and imparted his ebullience and understanding of the foods and culture of southern Italy. Franco and Gwen Romagnoli shared their recipes with me. I was also provided assistance and advice from Nancy Civetta, Corby Kummer, Rene Becker, and Elizabeth Constanza. My sister, Jane Silver, was a tireless traveling companion and supporter. And I owe countless thanks to Noelle Blanchard for tasting and testing recipes, and even more for her warm friendship.

This project couldn't have happened without my agent, Jane Dystel, whose skill and insight were essential in bringing this book into being. And I am indebted to my editors at Rodale, who have all been enthusiastic and creative.

And finally, I owe immeasurable appreciation to my husband David and daughters Annie and Rachel for their unwavering enthusiasm, support, and encouragement, their eagerness to accompany me on my eating adventures, and their willingness to eat whatever I cook.

INTRODUCTION

As enduring as the Italian landscape, *fagioli*—in all their different shapes, colors, and sizes—have been a cornerstone of the cuisine of Italy for thousands of years. Long before beans became an essential ingredient of the cooking of the Roman Empire, they provided sustenance and sustainable agriculture to the ancient civilizations that inhabited the Italian peninsula. But while the Roman appetite and culture was inclined to all types of beans, in the centuries that followed, legumes lost their luster and fell from favor. The final blow came during the Renaissance of the 1400s, when Catherine de' Medici attempted to refine Italian cooking along the lines of royal French cuisine. Beans of all varieties came to be regarded as peasant fare. They were disdained as "the meat of the poor."

It's been a long road back to respectability. But today, for just about everyone everywhere in Italy, *fagioli* are as essential as they are enjoyable, as fundamental as eating pasta, and an indispensable part of Italian cuisine.

My passion for the bean cuisine of Italy began almost 20 years ago, when I started traveling throughout the Italian peninsula to write about the foods I encountered there. At first, I was taken in by the bean soups, the robust, rich *minestrone,* and *pasta e fagioli.* Over time, I discovered more about the differences among the families of *fagioli* and savored their delicious distinctions, various and unique flavors and textures, and the remarkable diversity of bean preparations. I began to appreciate the bean as an ingredient of stature that deserves as much consideration in selection and preparation as the fresh produce I spend hours each week procuring from farm stands and markets.

The idea for this book crystallized after a number of visits with good friends at their house on the coast of Tuscany. We eat fresh beans almost daily in the summertime there, thanks to their greengrocer, Maria, who still grows most of what she sells in her shop. Maria likes you to buy—not necessarily what you came in for—her pick of the choicest vegetables she gathered in the early morning darkness and carried into town. That usually includes a sackful of fresh shell beans, always white *fagioli* of some variety, in their yellowish green pods, that are inseparable from Tuscan cuisine. Maria's fresh beans, and the superb ways in which our hosts prepared them, put me firmly on the path of *Fagioli: The Bean Cuisine of Italy.*

As one of the least expensive forms of protein, beans are as nutritious as they are practical, which is why they are an integral part of cultures all over the globe. Ounce for ounce, some beans have as much protein as a comparable amount of meat. And most beans can be either eaten fresh or dried and stored for months. The United States is one of the largest producers of beans in the world. But we are still not a nation of bean eaters. The preponderance of what we grow is soybeans that are processed in foods or exported. The result is that fresh beans are largely unavailable, and you'll find remarkably few bean dishes and hardly any that are memorable in American cooking.

By comparison, Italy grows most of its beans for local consumption—fresh beans in the summer and dried in the winter—and there are hundreds of bean recipes from nearly every region. You'll find beans in antipasti, salads, and side dishes; in soups; with pasta, polenta, barley, risotto, and *farro;* as well as in hearty main-course dishes prepared with everything from sausages, game, beef, lamb, and pork to fish and seafood. I have selected an encompassing range of recipes, all from Italian sources, that will let you experience the variety and versatility that characterize the Italian way with beans.

Bean Basics, the first chapter, provides the essential information you need to know about *fagioli.* You'll find a guide to the most common beans in Italy and their American counterparts so you can make substitutions when necessary. These include the numerous varieties of white beans such as cannellini (white kidney beans), chickpeas, fava beans, lentils, and *borlotti.* I have also covered some lesser-known, but popular, beans, as well as historical observations, nutritional facts, and cooking directions. In the Ingredient Guide, I have compiled information on the special Italian or hard-to-find ingredients: what they are and sources where you can purchase them if they are not available in your area, so you can successfully prepare the recipes.

The bean dishes of Italy offer a wealth of warm, wonderful foods that can be informally enjoyed by you, your family, and friends, whether there are two or twenty at the table. I hope that you will come along and share with me my affection and appreciation for *fagioli* and the bean cuisine of Italy.

BEAN BASICS

Beans belong to the family of leguminous, podded plants that also includes lentils and peas. The beans are the seeds of their plants and can be eaten raw from the pod, cooked, or dried for storage and cooked at a later point in time. Legumes are the third largest of all flowering plant groups, after daisies and orchids, and were among the first edible vegetation, along with grains, to be domesticated almost 10,000 years ago with the beginning of agriculture. The name *legume* comes from the Latin *legumen* or *legere,* "to gather." As the richest source of vegetable protein, and possessing the unique ability to enrich the soil that they grow in—whereas all other plants deplete the soil—legumes were cultivated and coveted in most early civilizations.

It is widely believed that lentils were the first legumes grown for human consumption. They appeared first in the Middle East and Southwest Asia and eventually in India and Eastern Europe. Egypt was, at one time, the largest exporter of lentils in the ancient world, and Italy was the major importer. The obelisk that stands in St. Peter's Square in Rome today was brought there from Egypt in A.D. 37, packed in a crate of lentils. This clever technique is used even today. Arthur Schwartz, a cookbook author and host of the New York City radio show *Food Talk,* says that he often sends home his pottery purchases from Italy protectively cushioned in lentils.

The fava bean, cultivated several thousand years after the

lentil, became one of the most important beans in the Roman Empire. It was valued both as a culinary staple and as a cultural token and was associated with many social customs and superstitions. Beans signified regeneration. Fava beans were ritual offerings to both marriage ceremonies—with each bean representing a male child in whom an ancestor would return to ensure the continuation of the family line—and funerals. In death, wrote Pliny, the ancient Roman writer and philosopher, fava beans withheld the souls of the dead.

Today, there are still remnants of myths about beans in contemporary Italian culture. Bianca Tragni, professor of Pugliese culture at the university in Altamura, writes in her book, *Altamura antichi sapori* (*Old Flavors of Altamura*), of several legends that involve beans or the names of beans. In one, a baby is so small, his mother calls him *chicco di lenticchie,* tiny lentil. In another, a version of the Ali Baba story, instead of "open sesame," the phrase is "open *cicerchie,*" which is a type of chickpea found mainly in Puglia.

By the end of the first century B.C., in addition to lentils and fava beans, there were numerous varieties of beans grown throughout the Italian peninsula. From several recipes recorded by Apicius, we know that the ancient Romans enjoyed a diversity of legumes. *Tisanum* was a stew of different legumes and vegetables that resembled the contemporary Sicilian and Calabrian soup *millecosedde* that is still prepared today. Legumes played such an important role in the Roman diet that several prominent families were named for specific beans: Fabius for the fava, Lentulus for the lentil, Pisolus for the pea. Cicero, one of the most distinguished Romans, got his name from the chickpea. The stories say that the reason the family was named for the chickpea was because Cicero's father had scarred, dimpled skin, like the surface of a chickpea.

The Beans of Italy

Today, Italians universally eat and enjoy beans. They are an essential part of the weekly meal cycle. Just as there are specific days when meat, fish, and pasta are served, in most families, there is always a day or two for beans.

To satisfy this national hunger, beans are grown throughout Italy. From the northern mountains of Piemonte and the Veneto to the southern island of Sicily, Italy produces thousands of tons of beans and legumes each year. Although Americans tend to group them all together, Italians make the distinction between beans, *fagioli,* and legumes, *legumi.* When I began working on this book and told Italian friends what I was doing, their response was, *"Solo fagioli?"* Only beans? How could there be a whole book on only beans, they asked? But when I added that the book would include recipes for lentils and chickpeas, *fagioli e legumi,* they were much more understanding and enthusiastic. Italians are always pleased when someone outside of Italy is interested in their cuisine.

Many bean growers I met in the course of writing this book are small family farmers who produce beans the way they have been grown and processed for hundreds of years. Enzo Pistelli's family has a *frantoio,* a small olive oil factory, and has been making olive oil for decades in Terni, in southern Umbria not far from Rome. Pistelli began growing beans several years ago on six hectares of rolling hills around his small factory. With a degree in agriculture from the university in Perugia, he was looking for a way to expand the family business. "Beans and olive oil go together," he said one day over a lunch of beans and olive oil, pecorino cheese, and prosciutto at his house. He cultivates a few varieties with great care. His beans are grown completely organically, using only natural manure as fertilizer. He air-dries the beans in their pods and has the dried beans shelled by hand.

Other small producers, like Mario Agostinelli in Regello, in the Pratomagno, the plain of central Tuscany southeast of Florence, are, like many family farms in the United States, growing heirloom varieties of several plants including beans. Eight years ago, he started cultivating the *zolfino,* a small white bean, and the *ceci rossa,* a diminutive chickpea, in an effort to revitalize these long-forgotten species.

In the summer and early fall, Italians enjoy their beans fresh from the shell—*fagioli sgranati*—lightly boiling them until they're tender and serving them with a little salt and olive oil. But they take equal care with their dried beans and legumes, *fagioli e legumi secchi,* the remainder of the year, soaking them overnight and gently simmering them until they become barely tender.

Italians don't keep dried beans in storage from one year to the next. In fact, many bean packages are sold with the *raccolto,* harvest date, printed on them to ensure buyers they are get-ting the "freshest" dried beans available. I discovered this at the end of August on one trip to Italy. I stopped by my favorite bean store, the Antica Bottega di Prospero, in Lucca, in Tuscany, to buy dried beans to bring home to Cambridge. But there were no local beans to be had. In the store, I found that the chickpeas and red kidney beans were from Mexico. And to my surprise, there weren't any Tuscan white cannellini beans. I think of cannellini as integral to Tuscan cooking and had assumed they could be bought throughout the year. But the shopkeeper explained that the new crop of dried beans from the summer harvest hadn't yet arrived, and last year's were sold out.

Throughout the various regions of the Italian peninsula, dozens of types of beans and legumes are grown. The most widely consumed are numerous variations of the *borlotti,* a red and tan speckled bean grown in the north; white beans, including cannellini, of which there are more than a dozen varieties from both the northern and southern regions; and the fava, which is typically found in the cooking of southern Italy and Sicily. Of the legumes, lentils, *lenticchie,* and chickpeas are the most popular.

Borlotti. Considered to be the most popular bean of northern Italy, *borlotti* (pronounced bor-LOH-tee) are regarded by many Italians to be the healthiest and most nutritious. With its high iron content, the *borlotti* is widely thought of as the best substitute for meat. Giovanella Giavazzi, a Milanese friend, recalls that when she was a child after World War II, her family would eat a soup of *borlotti* and pasta nearly every day because they couldn't afford meat. And Giovanni Bartolini, chef and owner of the restaurant La Luma in Montecossaro, in the Marches region, also told me that as a child he ate *borlotti* every other day as a nutritious alternative to meat.

Speckled in varying degrees of red, tan, and brown on the outside (like our pinto or cranberry beans), *borlotti,* when cooked, become a dark brown mahogany color on the outside and yellow on the inside. They have a deliciously creamy consistency. The town of Vigevano, southwest of Milan, is a center for *borlotti* cultivation. *Fagioli di Lamon,* which are grown in the area around the town of Lamon in the Veneto, look like a large cousin of the *borlotti.* But according to the official town lore, it's a distinct strain that was introduced to the area in the seventeenth century. Cuneo, a small city in Piemonte and a center of bean cultivation, also grows a *borlotti*-type bean called the *fagiolo di Cuneo.* The *borlottino* and *scozzesi* are similarly speckled beans grown elsewhere in Piemonte. The *borlotto di ceriana* is grown in the hills of Liguria, on the northern Mediterranean coast.

Cannellini. Tuscany is known as a bean-lover's paradise, and Tuscans are sometimes referred to as *mangia-fagioli,* or bean eaters. Cannellini (pronounced cah-neh-LEEN-ee), or white kidney beans, are probably the most closely associated with Tuscan cuisine. They are the only beans referred to simply as *fagioli*.

But the white beans of Tuscany are hardly limited to cannellini. They come in many shapes and sizes, from the small *soranini* and *toscanello* beans to the larger *corona* and *schiaccioni*. There are some strains, like the *sorana* from Montecarlo near Lucca and the *zolfino* from the Pratomagno, that are cultivated in such small quantities that you can find them only in the towns or areas where they are grown. White beans are not exclusive to Tuscany, however. In the hills of Liguria, overlooking the Mediterranean Sea, farmers grow three distinct but similar varieties of white beans: *fagioli di Conio, fagioli di Pigna,* and *fagioli di Badalucco.* All are larger and rounder than cannellini beans and are reputed to be the creamiest and tenderest white beans in all of Italy. But like the *sorana* bean of Tuscany, they're encountered only in the towns where they're grown, along the Ligurian coast. And in Piemonte, several varieties of white beans are grown, including *maomesi, spagna,* and *angolo.* In spite of this diversity, in most recipes calling for white beans, you can substitute one white bean for another as far as taste goes, but the difference in size and shape affects the texture and eating experience of any given dish.

Ceci. Chickpeas, or *ceci* (pronounced CHEH-chee), with their characteristic neutral tan color and almost round hazelnut-like shape, are familiar to most American cooks, but perhaps not as an Italian ingredient. Chickpeas are known here for their prevalence in Middle Eastern cuisine, specifically the dish hummus, which has become an American supermarket staple. But *ceci* are also an essential component of both southern and northern Italian cooking, where chickpeas are typically cooked in soups and other traditional dishes.

I always regarded the chickpea as a fairly standard item without much in the way of variation. But it turns out that numerous types are grown in Italy. There are smaller and larger versions as well as some unusual strains, such as the corn kernel–shaped *cicerchie* (pronounced chee-CHAIR-kee-ay). Smaller ones come from Umbria and larger ones from Puglia. Lately, black chickpeas—the ones you usually pick out and throw away—have become popular in better restaurants. Rosella Speranza, who lives in Bari and is a promoter of Pugliese culture and cuisine, told me how as a child, her mother would use the black chickpeas as chicken feed. Today, however, they're sold in chic *gastronomie,* gourmet food shops. Chickpeas are also the source of chickpea flour, *farina di ceci,* used to prepare the traditional Ligurian snack *farinata.*

In *Honey from a Weed,* English writer Patience Gray chronicles her experiences living and eating in Italy. She describes fresh chickpeas as brilliant green in color and tasting of lemon.

Favas. Integral to the cuisine of the southern Italian regions of Abruzzo, Puglia, Campania, and Sicily, favas (pronounced FAH-vah) are eaten fresh and dried. The fava, or broad bean, as it is frequently called in the United States, is probably the hardiest of all the beans and legumes grown anywhere. It is typically planted in November and harvested in April, the reverse of the other, more delicate bean varieties. This hardiness is due in part to the fava's double shell: Favas have an outer pod, and each bean is held within an inner protective seed cover, or skin. These should be peeled on dried and fresh favas alike, except for the youngest, smallest, freshest ones.

When you buy dried fava beans, you'll have two options: either whole, with their protective skins (called *fave con la buccia*), or skinned and split (called *fave bianche,* because the skinned favas are yellow-white in color). With the skins on, dried favas are formidable to prepare. The brownish green skin is fairly tough, and even after hours of soaking and cooking, it does not become tender. Although it does not make dried favas inedible, the skin lends the cooked beans a subtle bitter taste and gives whatever dish they're prepared in a rough, rustic texture. Whole dried favas also have a black seed that looks like it's sewn into the edge of the bean. It should be cut out after soaking and before cooking, adding yet another step in the preparation.

Skinned, split favas are much less work, requiring no soaking and readily becoming soft and tender when cooked. They are sold in Italian specialty food shops, but are also widely and inexpensively available in Middle Eastern food stores (see Ingredient Guide on page 19).

Fresh fava beans are typically found in specialty produce shops and ethnic food markets in the early spring. Each long, fat pod usually contains about six beans. The smallest, greenest beans don't require attention beyond cooking or blanching and dressing in a salad. The larger ones, however, are best when the outer skin is peeled from the bean. Although it's not essential to peel the skin from fresh favas, I think they taste better and look better, as they keep their green color during cooking. Peeling is easy because the skin is fairly loose and comes off with a little help from a sharp paring knife or your fingernail. About 1½ to 2 pounds of whole fava beans in their pods yield approximately 1 cup of shelled beans.

Lenticchie. Lentils, or *lenticchie* (pronounced len-TEE-kee-ay), are eaten all over Italy. The choicest, and most expensive, are grown in Umbria, Abruzzo, and Sicily. The best Italian lentils are small and brown. They have a deliciously nutty taste and hold their shape during cooking. Larger brown varieties like our American-grown lentils are also grown in Italy. In one bean shop I visited, they were even labeled *lenticchie Americane.* In all the recipes in this book calling for lentils, I recommend using Italian small brown lentils, if possible. Good substitutes are green French lentils, because they're similarly small and flavorful and retain their firm, round shape during cooking. These are widely available in many large supermarkets as well as specialty food shops. Although lentils do not require soaking before cooking, many Italian cooks soak their lentils, from as little as 1 hour to up to 24 hours, depending on the cook and the recipe.

In addition to these major groups of beans, Italians grow and cook with split peas, *piselli;* black-eyed peas, *fagioli dell'occhio;* and red kidney beans, called either *fagioli rossi, fagioli rossi lucchesi,* or *fagioli messicani,* depending on where they are found. As evidence of globalization, you can now find soybeans, called *soya,* azuki beans, and mung beans in most Italian bean shops, but they are not grown in Italy and are not traditional ingredients.

The Bean Chart

The following chart is designed to help you select dried beans that are widely available in American food stores if you cannot obtain the Italian varieties either from local specialty markets or from mail-order or Internet sources (see Ingredient Guide on page 19 for sources). When I discovered that white beans for sale in a shop in Florence, labeled *fagioli pisani,* were in fact Great Northern beans from Canada, I decided that if Italian cooks could use an American bean, so could we.

I strongly recommend buying beans from a reliable source where there is ample turnover of the product. I agree with Italian cooks: The fresher the dried bean, the better it will taste. Beans that still have some moisture in the center conduct heat more evenly and efficiently.

BEAN/LEGUME	COLOR AND SHAPE	SUBSTITUTES
BORLOTTI	RED AND TAN SPECKLED, MEDIUM KIDNEY SHAPE	PINTO, CRANBERRY
CANNELLINI	WHITE, MEDIUM KIDNEY SHAPE	GREAT NORTHERN
CHICKPEA	TAN, ROUNDISH	NO SUBSTITUTE
CICERCHIE	TAN, CORN KERNEL SHAPE	CHICKPEA
CORONA	WHITE, EXTRA-LARGE OVAL	CANNELLINI
FAGIOLO COCO	WHITE, OVAL	CANNELLINI, GREAT NORTHERN
FAGIOLI DI LAMON	RED AND TAN SPECKLED, LARGE KIDNEY SHAPE	BORLOTTI, PINTO, CRANBERRY
FAGIOLI DI PIGNA, DI CONIO, DI BADALUCCO	WHITE, MEDIUM OVAL	CANNELLINI, GREAT NORTHERN
FAGIOLI DEL PURGATORIO	WHITE, EXTRA-SMALL OVAL	NAVY BEANS
FAGIOLI ROSSI	RED, KIDNEY SHAPE	RED KIDNEY BEANS
FAVA BEANS, SKINNED, SPLIT	YELLOW, FLAT, THIN, OVAL	NO SUBSTITUTE
FAVA BEANS, WHOLE	BROWN, LARGE OVAL	NO SUBSTITUTE
LENTICCHIE	BROWN, SMALL DISK SHAPE	FRENCH GREEN LENTILS
ROMAN	RED AND TAN SPECKLED, MEDIUM KIDNEY SHAPE	BORLOTTI, PINTO, CRANBERRY
SORANINI, TOSCANELLO, ZOLFINO	WHITE, SMALL OVAL	GREAT NORTHERN, NAVY BEAN

Cooking Guide

While you may never find two Italian cooks who agree on the ingredients in *pasta e fagioli,* every Italian cook I spoke with agreed on the proper way to cook beans: slowly and gently. So moderately, in fact, that you can barely detect the beans are simmering when you look into the pot. That way, the beans don't break or turn to mush during cooking.

Some Italian cooks still use a traditional terra-cotta bean pot, called a *fagioliera* in Tuscany and a *pignata* in Puglia, because it does the job perfectly. But today, most are more likely to use a conventional pot. Whatever pot you do use, beans should be softly simmered, never rapidly boiled, until they reach the desired degree of doneness. Cooking time can vary from about 30 minutes to 1½ hours, depending on the age and the type of bean. It's not surprising that so many Americans think of beans as a bland, starchy component in soups, stews, and chili. That's the way they're prepared in most American recipes. But Italian cooks know how to make beans invitingly tender, not too soft, and surprisingly flavorful. And with a little know-how and planning, you can too.

When figuring quantities, in general, you can assume that 1 cup of dried beans will yield about 2 cups of cooked beans.

Soaking beans. With the exception of lentils, split peas, and dried, skinned, split favas, all dried beans should be soaked for 8 hours or longer. Before soaking, it's always a good idea to pick through the beans and remove any that are discolored or broken. Soaking provides a preliminary softening of the exterior wall of the beans and enables them to cook relatively quickly. Soaking also reveals a lot about the age and dryness of the beans. Beans that float or shrivel are probably damaged or very old. They may not cook evenly.

Soaking time directly affects cooking time. The more time you soak beans, up to a point, the less cooking time is required. If you don't soak the beans at all or don't soak them long enough, you will have to cook them that much longer. On the other hand, oversoaking—for more than 24 hours—isn't advisable either, because beans begin to ferment. Chickpeas won't ever become tender unless they are soaked in advance of cooking. If you plan ahead and soak the beans overnight or begin to soak them first thing in the morning, you can easily prepare most of the recipes in this book in a reasonable amount of time for dinner that night. Some Italian cooks swear by the addition of baking soda in the soaking water to ensure that the beans don't break apart during cooking, but I haven't found this to yield significantly better results than gentle simmering.

To soak, place the dried beans in a large bowl with an ample amount of cold water to cover and allow to stand at room temperature for 8 hours or longer. You can speed up the soaking process and cut the soaking time by about half by using hot or boiling water instead of cold water. The soaking water should always be drained and discarded before cooking beans. This helps reduce or eliminate any digestive reactions to beans (see Health and Nutrition on page 17). Once the beans are drained of their soaking water, rinse them under cold water and allow them to drain again.

Cooking beans. When cooking beans, use plenty of water to allow room for expansion: 6 cups of water for every cup of beans, except in those recipes such as soups that require a specific amount of water. To give beans flavor, many Italian cooks add onions, carrots, celery, and garlic to the pot with the beans. In northern Italy, various herbs, such as sage, rosemary, or bay leaf, are added either individually or in combinations. In southern Italy, as in Puglia, where the cuisine was traditionally a *cucina povera,* poor cooking, beans used to be cooked in plain water, although cooks today are likely to add a bay leaf and a clove of garlic. My personal preference is to use a whole clove of garlic with the papery white skin on and a sprig of rosemary or a few sage leaves or a bay leaf. I also often add a tablespoon or more of olive oil to the cooking water. This both flavors the beans and prevents them from sticking together. It's best to avoid adding salt to the beans until they are done, as it will retard the cooking process and can prevent the beans from becoming completely tender. I like to cook beans until they are tender, but not so soft that they fall apart.

For cooking, place soaked, drained beans in a heavy medium (3- to 4-quart) saucepan. Add 6 cups cold water for every cup of beans and place over medium-high heat. Bring the water to a boil. Lower the heat to medium-low and simmer gently, uncovered, until tender.

Cooking times. Cooking times will vary depending on the type of bean. Use this chart as a guide (all times are approximate).

BORLOTTI, FAGIOLI DI LAMON, PINTO, CRANBERRY	1 HOUR
BLACK-EYED PEAS	30 TO 45 MINUTES
CANNELLINI	1 HOUR
CHICKPEAS, CICERCHIE	1 TO 1½ HOURS
FAVA BEANS—WHOLE, WITH SKINS	1 TO 1½ HOURS
FAVA BEANS—YELLOW, SKINNED, SPLIT	30 TO 45 MINUTES
GREAT NORTHERN, SORANINI, TOSCANELLO	1 HOUR
LENTILS	30 TO 45 MINUTES

Once the beans are cooked, I like to leave them in their cooking water until I am ready to use them, whether it's an hour or a day later. I find this improves their flavor. Plus, the *brodo,* cooking water, is very tasty and is often added at least in part to soups, stews, and many pasta dishes. It should not go to waste. When I cook beans a day or more in advance, I leave them in their cooking water, allow to cool, and refrigerate, broth and all, until I am ready to use them. If I have beans left over that have been drained, I store them in a plastic container, covered with fresh water, in the refrigerator. I don't keep the cooked beans for more than 2 days before using them.

Cooking beans in a pressure cooker. A fast way to soak and cook beans is to use a pressure cooker. It cuts the soaking and cooking times dramatically and preserves the nutrients in the beans, since almost nothing cooks away. But as much as I like using a pressure cooker to prepare many dishes, I have found significant drawbacks to pressure-cooking beans, and I don't generally recommend it for preparing most of the recipes in this book. Cooking under pressure increases the cooking temperature inside the cooker. As a result, the beans cook at a very high temperature very rapidly—the opposite of how beans should be cooked according to Italian recipes for the most flavor and best texture. I also find that pressure-cooking often yields uneven results. From one pot of beans, some will be overdone, split apart, and broken, and others underdone, still hard and crunchy. The only occasion when I can recommend a pressure cooker is when you are preparing beans for one of the spreads for *crostini* (see pages 32–40) or for the *passati,* pureed soups, because the overcooking won't adversely affect the finished results.

When using a pressure cooker, always follow the manufacturer's directions and never fill the cooker more than two-thirds full.

To soak beans in a pressure cooker, add the beans to the pot with just enough water to cover. Close the cooker according to the manufacturer's directions and bring the pressure up to full. Cook for 5 minutes, then bring the pressure down immediately by placing the cooker in the sink and running cold water over the top until the safety features indicate that the pressure has dropped and it is safe to open the cover. Drain the beans, discard the cooking water, and rinse.

Return the beans to the pressure cooker and add at least 6 cups of cold water for every cup of dried beans. Follow the manufacturer's directions for using the pressure cooker. Close the cooker, bring the pressure up to full, and start timing the cooking as soon as the pressure has reached its maximum point, according to the manufacturer's directions. Beans will be done in from 10 to 20 minutes, depending on the type of bean. When cooking is complete, immediately bring the pressure down again using the cold water method described above. Drain the beans in a colander.

Canned or store-bought beans. Some recipes in this book call for cooked beans. Although it's always better to cook your own, convenience may occasionally lead you to substitute store-bought for home-cooked. In general, if you do choose canned beans, I recommend using one of the organic brands, such as Health Valley, from natural food stores. In my experience, the organic brands are better: not overcooked and mushy, and not salted. Always drain and rinse beans from a can in a strainer before using, and allow them to stand and drain for several minutes to eliminate any excess water.

Not all recipes are easily altered to accommodate canned beans. In many recipes, beans and their cooking liquid are essential to the preparation. When it is possible to substitute canned beans, skip the soaking and cooking steps, and for every cup of dried beans called for, you can substitute 2 cups canned beans.

Health and Nutrition

Notwithstanding the esteem the Romans had for their legumes, in the centuries since the Roman Empire fell, beans have had a humble, impoverished, and often maligned image. That image stands in stark contrast to the nutritional and health benefits that can be gained from a diet rich in beans and legumes. Beans are among the world's most valuable foods for human consumption and have been shown to improve overall health in a number of significant ways.

- Beans are high in both soluble and insoluble types of fiber. It has been demonstrated that a diet that contains a significant amount of fiber can help reduce the risk of coronary heart disease, improve bowel function, and help prevent colon cancer.

- Like oats and oat products, beans can help reduce serum cholesterol levels.

- Beans are considered to be "good" carbohydrates with low glycemic levels. The glycemic index of particular foods relates to the carbohydrates and how quickly or slowly they are metabolized. Beans and other carbohydrates with low glycemic levels are digested slowly. Therefore, they aid in weight control, providing a feeling of fullness and helping to reduce fat absorption in the body. In addition, foods with low glycemic levels can help prevent diabetes in those who are at risk for developing the disease.

- Beans are rich in protein, containing the highest amount of protein of any vegetable. In fact, gram for gram, some bean varieties have as much protein as chicken or other meats. Fava beans and lentils are composed of 25 percent protein, peas 24 percent, and chickpeas 21 percent. White, speckled, and kidney beans all contain approximately 22 percent. And when beans are combined with grain in the diet, their protein becomes even more accessible and valuable nutritionally.

- ꝏ Beans contain valuable micronutrients, phytoceuticals, B vitamins, and iron, as well as zinc, calcium, and small amounts of folate (folic acid), potassium, and magnesium.

There are, however, health complications that may come with beans. The most severe is a condition called favism. Although it affects only a small number of people, it comes from ingesting fresh, uncooked fava beans, which can cause hemolytic anemia with symptoms of severe jaundice and anemia. For most of us, though, the worst that can happen from eating beans is bloating, gas, or other gastric symptoms that sometimes accompany digestion. While many individual and variable characteristics can lead to these symptoms, what essentially accounts for gastric distress are the carbohydrates—the strands of sugar molecules, or oligosaccharides, of which beans and legumes are composed—that our bodies have a hard time digesting. Because these carbohydrates cannot be satisfactorily broken down by our enzymes in the upper digestive tract, they become extra work for the lower digestive area. That extra work leads to digestive symptoms. My own experience has demonstrated that it is possible to avoid any or all discomfort after eating beans with proper preparation and cooking. Always discard the water the beans soak in and always thoroughly cook the beans. Undercooked beans create even more work for the digestive system. In addition, there are products on the market, such as Beano, that can be taken with a meal of beans to avoid gastric distress.

INGREDIENT GUIDE

Most of the ingredients called for in this book are standard supermarket items and should be available in your area. Some of the Italian or less familiar ingredients, however, may have to be obtained from mail-order sources. Following is a guide to identifying and locating the specialty Italian items and many of the basic ingredients. Italian cooking and recipes are rarely complicated. But the freshest possible produce and particular condiments, seasonings, and flavorings are essential if you want to experience Italian food as it tastes in Italy.

Anchovies. Salted anchovies, *acciughe* or *alici,* are by far the best, most flavorful, and most desirable to use in cooking. Their heads are already removed when they're packed, but they do require rinsing, to remove the salt, and filleting, which can easily be done with your fingers or with a paring knife. Even though it's extra work, they're worth it for their deliciously fishy taste. After you open a can of salted anchovies, they will keep in the refrigerator and be usable for several months. However, if you're planning to keep them for a while, it's advisable to transfer the anchovies to a glass or plastic container with a tight-fitting lid.

Unsalted anchovies packed in oil, which are more common and more convenient, are also fine to use in these recipes, but you'll typically have to use double the amount to achieve the same flavor you'd get from salted anchovies. Small jars of anchovies in oil are available in most supermarkets as well as specialty food stores. Cans of salted anchovies are available from www.agferrari.com.

Beans. *Fagioli* and *legumi* (dried beans) from Italy—including *borlotti, fagioli di Lamon,* cannellini, *ceci, cicerchie, fave, fagioli del purgatorio,* and lentils, among other varieties—are available from several sources: Formaggio Kitchen in Cambridge, Massachusetts (888-212-3224) as well as www.agferrari.com, www.pastacheese.com, and www.chefshop.com. Formaggio Kitchen is the sole American importer for the Pistelli Umbrian beans, including lentils, *cicerchie,* and *fagioli del purgatorio.* Prices for dried beans from Italy vary from about $5 to $8 a pound, depending on the particular beans, whether they're organic, whether they're processed by hand, and who the packager is in Italy. These sources also carry some Italian beans in cans.

You may find dried beans from Italy in Italian specialty food shops in your area. Some natural food stores, such as Whole Foods Markets, offer a small selection of imported beans, including whole fava beans in their skins, in addition to a wide selection of organically grown beans from the United States.

Dried split, skinned fava beans imported from Italy are widely imported from the Middle East and are generally available in Middle Eastern food markets.

American-grown varieties of Italian beans including *borlotti* and cannellini are available from www.beanbag.net and www.purcellmountainfarms.com.

For a complete description of the individual beans, see Bean Basics on page 1.

Bottarga. *Bottarga* is the preserved roe from tuna or mullet. It is removed as soon as the fish is caught, then salted, pressed into a cake, and smoked. It's a luxury item, at over $40 a half pound, but it's worth it for its incomparable delicate fish taste. It comes both grated and whole. For the Salad of White Beans and Bottarga (see page 60), you'll need the whole roe cake, which you slice yourself. *Bottarga* from Sardinia tends to be a little less expensive than the *bottarga* from Sicily. I've rarely encountered it in food shops, and only in Manhattan. I order it online from www.esperya.com.

Broth. The best broth is the kind you make yourself. But most of us find ourselves turning to store-bought broth at one time or another. My own particular favorite is the shelf-stabilized box of fat-free chicken broth offered by Health Valley or Trader Joe's. They also make a vegetable broth and a free-range chicken broth. What makes these broths appealing is their subtle flavoring. You want a broth that will add body and enhance the tastes of the dish you are preparing. You don't want an overly seasoned broth that will overwhelm what you're cooking. And you want to avoid salty broth prepared from bouillon powder or cubes.

Cheeses. The cheeses called for in the recipes in this book include *parmigiano-reggiano* (referred to as simply *parmigiano*) and *grana padano* (a cheese similar in both taste and appearance to *parmigiano* but made in a different area of Italy). In addition, several sheep's-milk grating cheeses are called for, including *pecorino romano, pecorino sardo,* and *pecorino toscano. Pecorino romano* and *pecorino sardo* are from southern Italy, while *pecorino toscano* is from Tuscany. The *pecorino* from southern Italy will have a saltier, stronger flavor than the *pecorino* from Tuscany.

For the best flavor, it's always best to buy a piece of cheese and grate your own. You will usually get some rind with your piece of cheese. You should save the *parmigiano* rind to add to soups (see Genoa-Style Minestrone with Pesto on page 96). Alternatively, shops that freshly grate cheese will often have pieces of rind to sell.

Another cheese called for in the recipes is *mascarpone*. It is a fresh cow's-milk cheese that's similar to sour cream or crème fraîche.

These cheeses are available in many supermarkets and specialty food shops. In addition, there are several good online sources for Italian cheeses, including www.todarobros.com, www.murrayscheese.com, and www.pastacheese.com. Or you can call Formaggio Kitchen (888-212-3224).

Chickpea flour. Essential for the preparation of the Ligurian specialty *farinata*, chickpea flour is available from some natural food stores, including Whole Foods Markets, Middle Eastern specialty food shops, and online from www.todarobros.com.

Farro. Also called spelt, *farro* is a variety of hard wheat that has been cultivated in Italy since the time of ancient Rome. It is grown in Tuscany near Lucca, in Umbria, and in the Marches regions. It has a deliciously nutty flavor and wonderful texture that is somewhat chewy after it's cooked. *Farro* can be bought in many Italian specialty shops as well as in the Whole Foods chain of supermarkets, which sells it in vacuum-sealed bags. You can also find *farro* online at www.pastacheese.com, and www.agferrari.com. It's available in bulk from Formaggio Kitchen (888-212-3224).

Game meats. Game including duck, squab, partridge, pheasant, and goose is available from www.dartagnan.com.

Garlic. Garlic is one of the most basic and essential ingredients in Italian cuisine. I have two basic principles when it comes to garlic. The first is: Whenever possible, use the freshest garlic you can buy. With the proliferation of farmers' markets and the availability of fresh produce direct from the fields, I've come to treasure the super-fresh and highly flavored garlic varieties that I can buy during the growing season in the Northeast. During the winter, I like to go to ethnic markets, where fresh garlic is considered an important staple and where they often have higher-quality bulbs than I can find elsewhere. The fresher the garlic, the less bitter and the less overpowering the flavor. Fresher garlic is also less likely to cause bad breath. You can easily identify older garlic: The white papery outer layers are dry and falling off; sometimes whole cloves compress into dust when you exert any pressure on the bulb with your fingers; or cloves have sprouting roots. On the other hand, really fresh garlic will be firm from the outside in. Outer layers aren't dry and papery but have a skin so tight that the cloves are difficult to peel; the cloves are juicy when you cut them and have a clean taste whether they're cooked or eaten raw.

The second principle I follow for garlic is to steer clear of the garlic press and always chop garlic with a knife. I used to be a garlic-press user. I didn't appreciate that there could be a difference in taste between pressing or chopping it; pressing is a lot faster. But I've come to know for certain that while pressed garlic may be a time-saver, chopped garlic is more pleasant to eat. Pressed garlic tends to leave a strong, bitter taste, while chopped garlic delicately flavors without any unpalatable side effects.

Large heads of garlic are appealing because it's easier to peel the bigger cloves. But I find that smaller heads with more diminutive cloves, especially those with skins tinged purple and red, often have the best flavor.

In Italy, a clove of garlic that goes into a pot of beans is usually added *in camice,* literally "in the shirt," with its skin left on.

Guanciale. *Guanciale* (GWAN-cha-lay) is cured (not smoked) pork jowl, a fatty cut from the cheek of the pig. It is a specialty of Rome, and it may be used as a substitute for pancetta (see page 26). It's an unusual product in the United States, even in Italian specialty food shops. *Guanciale* is available by mail order from Salumeria Biellese in New York City (212-736-7376), Formaggio Kitchen (888-212-3224), and www.nimanranch.com.

Lentils. Italian lentils are typically small and brown. The finest ones come from Umbria, Abruzzo, and Sicily. They hold their shape during cooking and have a delicate, nutty lentil flavor. Italy also produces large brown lentils, like our American-grown brown lentils, but I don't recommend these for the recipes in this book. A good substitute for the small Italian lentils is the French green lentils. The taste is similar, and they also hold their shape when cooked. (For sources, see Beans on page 20.)

Mushrooms. From the mountains in the north of Italy to the forests in the south, Italy is a land of myriad wild mushroom varieties. And *funghi porcini,* with their fat stems and full round caps, are the most abundant of all the wild mushrooms harvested there. The name is derived from the squat, plump shape of the mushrooms: *funghi* means "mushrooms"; *porcini,* "little pigs." Fresh, they are a common sight in markets during the cooler, rainier months. But the Italian passion for mushrooms isn't limited to what's available in the markets. Italians are well-known for mushroom foraging.

While fresh wild mushrooms are an essential part of Italian cuisine, fresh *funghi porcini* are almost never available in the United States. They're rarely exported, as they deteriorate rapidly, and local specimens rarely make it to food stores. But the lack of fresh wild mushrooms shouldn't deter you from preparing any of the recipes calling for *funghi porcini.* Dried porcini are widely exported and available, although they can be costly. With cost and quality in mind, some caution should be taken when buying dried *funghi porcini.*

There are several grades of dried *funghi porcini,* and unless you know what to look for, you may end up paying a lot for an inferior product. In food markets in Italy, where the dried mushrooms are laid out according to their quality in piles in the various stalls, you can see clearly what distinguishes the most expensive mushrooms from the least expensive. The best dried mushrooms are mostly whitish pieces of carefully sliced caps. As you work your way down the price scale, the dried pieces become smaller, and there are fewer sliced caps and more sliced stems. Although you can cook with any of the dried mushrooms, the higher the quality of the dried mushrooms, the better the flavor will be. Since dried *funghi porcini* are al-

most always sold already packaged in the United States, you should look carefully at the specimens within the packaging to see, as best you can, what you're paying for. Good-quality dried *funghi porcini* from Italy are available online at www.chefshop.com and www.myspicer.com.

A cooking tip on dried *funghi porcini:* Always soak them in warm, not hot or boiling, water. Boiling water leaches most of the flavor out into the water, leaving the mushrooms tasteless.

Olive oil. Olive oil is one of the three principal building blocks of Italian cooking, along with garlic and salt. Pure olive oil is most widely used in cooking; the best extra virgin oil is reserved for salad dressings or for garnishing soups.

Italian cooks don't measure olive oil by the teaspoon, the tablespoon, or even the generous cup. It is used abundantly from a bottle, by the pour. Measurements are strictly by eyesight. Italian recipes typically call for "olive oil"—cooks can add as much or as little as they like. I've come to rely on my bottle-stopper spouts—the kind used in bars to measure out drinks from the liquor bottles—for pouring olive oil. They enable me to control the flow of the oil. I have given exact quantities for my recipes, but you can always add more or less to your taste. In addition to the oil used in preparing the recipes, many dishes call for a "drizzle" of olive oil as a garnish over each serving. That means just a little pour or a teaspoon of your best extra virgin olive oil dripped over the top of the dish. Italians call this a *filo*. Literally translated, it means "thread."

Olive oil is available in supermarkets everywhere. If you're looking for olive oil from a particular region of Italy, you can find a good selection online from www.agferrari.com.

One particularly flavorful brand is Pistelli olive oil from Umbria. Pistelli oil and beans are available via e-mail from frantoiopistelli@virgilio.it and also from Formaggio Kitchen (888-212-3224).

Pancetta. A cured meat, very much like bacon, pancetta is cut from the belly of the pig. It is traditionally cured in salt and uncooked. Occasionally, you will find smoked or spiced pancetta, but I don't recommend these for the recipes in this book. The exception is *Jota* (see page 228), a main-course soup from Friuli that calls for smoked pancetta.

Pancetta is a basic ingredient in Italian cooking. Along with onions, carrots, and celery, it forms the *soffritto,* the primary flavoring, in countless dishes. There are two styles of pancetta: *arrotolata* (rolled) and *stesa* (slab). Rolled pancetta tends to be more lean. You can order most types of pancetta from Formaggio Kitchen (888-212-3224).

Parsley. Not surprisingly, the parsley of choice for all the recipes in this book is flat-leaf "Italian" parsley. Italian recipes traditionally measure parsley not by the tablespoon or quarter cup but by the stem, even though only the leaves are used. It makes sense because the more you chop parsley, the less volume you have. The stems, which usually have three branches of leaves, are eventually discarded or saved for preparing stock. The leaves are picked from the stems and chopped. I have followed the Italian approach and called for parsley stems in the lists of ingredients for the recipes. Remember to use only the leaves.

Pasta. Whenever possible, use imported Italian pasta. It is made with hard durum wheat and will provide both the flavor and the texture essential for Italian recipes. There are many imported brands available in the big supermarket chains as well as small specialty food shops. I use whatever brand I can find that has the shape I'm looking for. Some of the best brands include Latini, Rustichella d'Abruzzo, and Benito Cellini. Good sources for Italian pasta online are www.pastacheese.com and www.agferrari.com.

When cooking pasta, always add salt to the water. Italians use a generous amount of salt in cooking and especially in their pasta water. I like to add at least a tablespoon of salt to a pot of water for cooking pasta.

Always cook your pasta in an abundant amount of water. When there is too little water, it takes longer for the pasta to cook, which can adversely affect the pasta's texture.

You can figure out what shape pasta to use by what kind of sauce or dish you're preparing. When preparing pasta with beans, you want the pasta to fit the sauce or the soup. Pasta and bean dishes usually call for short shapes of pasta: *tubetti, ditalini, conchigliette, orecchiette, pennette, cavatellini*. When long strands such as spaghetti or *fettuccine* are called for, you must first break the strands into smaller pieces.

Polenta. Polenta is cornmeal. You can use American milled cornmeal, but I like to use Italian polenta. Whichever nationality you choose, the kind with the most flavor is actually stone-ground. You can order Italian polenta from For-maggio Kitchen (888-212-3224), www.todarobros.com, and www.agferrari.com. Here's my basic recipe for polenta.

Basic Polenta

1   cup yellow polenta,
     preferably stone-ground
1   tablespoon salt

Put the polenta in a heavy 4-quart pot or casserole. Add the salt. Stirring constantly with a wire whisk, add 5 cups cold water to the pot with the polenta. Place the pot over medium heat. Continue to stir with the whisk until the polenta begins to thicken, about 10 minutes. Switch to a wooden spoon and continue to cook the polenta, stirring almost constantly, about 30 minutes longer. The polenta is done when it is thick but still pourable.

Makes 4 servings

Prosciutto. Called *prosciutto crudo,* or raw ham, prosciutto is not really "raw"; rather, it's cured, salted, and air-dried. It is made all over Italy, but there are two principal varieties that are imported into the United States: *prosciutto di Parma* from Emilia-Romagna and *prosciutto di San Daniele* from Friuli. Both are widely available. There are also comparable American-made versions that are easy to find and less expensive in many supermarkets, as well as in delicatessens and specialty shops. To my taste, the American varieties don't compare with the prosciutto from Italy. Make sure you do not buy smoked prosciutto or cooked prosciutto, as these will adversely affect the taste of a dish.

Rice. Italy grows many varieties of rice, both long and short grain. But it is the short-grain rice for risotto that I call for in the recipes in this book. Of these, arborio rice is the most widely available. Other types of Italian rice that you can find in the United States include *vialone nano* (which has a slightly smaller grain than arborio) and *carnaroli*. Any one of these can be used. You can also use American-grown arborio rice. But if you can find the Italian varieties, I recommend using them. To my taste, American rice is less starchy, and therefore, risotto prepared with it will be less creamy. Sources for Italian rice include www.agferrari.com, www.pastacheese.com, and Formaggio Kitchen (888-212-3224).

Sausages. There are so many sausage varieties in shops today that you can usually find one to suit your taste. However, for recipes in this book, I would avoid those with flavorings such as apples, maple, or sun-dried tomatoes. I like to use "sweet" Italian sausage—as opposed to the spicy, "hot" variety—and I prefer that it not be seasoned with fennel seed, a common ingredient. Wild boar and other game sausages are available from www.dartagnan.com and www.nimanranch.com. You can use ground pork in place of sausage.

Tomatoes. Fresh, juicy, flavorful tomatoes are a rarity, except in the summer or if you happen to live in a temperate climate where the growing season goes around the calendar. Because I live in the Northeast, I use cherry and fresh plum tomatoes in the few recipes that call for fresh tomatoes. These have good tomato flavor and don't require any peeling, making them very convenient. Otherwise, I use canned Italian plum tomatoes. Canned tomatoes should be cut open, seeded, and drained before they are chopped and added to a recipe. You can also buy cans or cartons of chopped or ground tomatoes, and I find them to be a convenient source much like the strained tomato puree that I call for in some of my recipes. Tomato paste, a concentrated form of tomato puree, is also widely available. When buying tomato paste, all brands are not the same. The taste varies from brand to brand. And some are available in cans, others in a tube. For convenience, I like to use the tube. I find that the Amore brand has the essence of tomato flavor, with a pleasant sharpness and rich taste.

Tuna. Tuna packed in olive oil, *tonno sott'olio,* is the best-tasting canned tuna around and should be used for preparing Italian recipes. I prefer it to any American tuna varieties, whether they are packed in oil or water. Most supermarkets carry at least one brand; Genoa and Progresso are two widely available labels you'll find in grocery stores. In specialty food shops, you may be able to find other brands. My choice, when I can find it, is Flott tuna from Sicily. It is available in smaller quantities in cans and in larger pieces in jars. All are packed in olive oil. You can order it from Formaggio Kitchen (888-212-3224) and www.todarobros.com. Several Web sites offer *ventresca* tuna, fillets cut from bluefin tuna, which costs upward of $20 a can, but it's delicious for a special salad. You can find it at www.vinoeolio.com and www.esperya.com.

An Italian meal is almost always served in several courses, and beans are as fundamental to the smaller, lighter first-course dishes as they are to the more robust soups and entrees. Beans are an excellent topping for *crostini* and *bruschetta,* and they become a magical ingredient in salads, *insalate,* blending seafood, greens, and vegetables into surprisingly savory and satisfying combinations. Salads are never served cold. They are customarily eaten at room temperature. Keep in mind that many of these recipes, including the side dishes, *contorni,* are versatile and can be served as a main course for lunch or a light supper.

Crostini di fagioli bianchi

WHITE BEAN SPREAD FOR CROSTINI

This versatile bean spread can be prepared well ahead of time, even a day or two. Remove the spread from the refrigerator an hour before you plan to serve it. Always serve at room temperature.

I like to accompany it with thinly sliced, crusty bread, crostini, that may be toasted or served fresh. You can improvise with this recipe and add more garlic or lemon juice or even some fresh parsley chopped in with the beans. Because the consistency of cooked beans varies, you can add some additional olive oil if the spread seems too thick or dry.

1 CUP DRIED WHITE BEANS, SUCH AS CANNELLINI OR GREAT NORTHERN, OR 2 CUPS COOKED WHITE BEANS, DRAINED

SALT

1 CLOVE GARLIC, OR MORE TO TASTE, PEELED

JUICE OF ½ LEMON

¼ CUP EXTRA VIRGIN OLIVE OIL, PLUS MORE FOR SERVING

FRESHLY GROUND BLACK PEPPER

1 LOAF FRENCH-STYLE BAGUETTE, SLICED INTO ¼-INCH-THICK SLICES, OR OTHER COUNTRY BREAD, CUT INTO SMALL SERVING-SIZE PIECES

If you are using dried beans, soak them in cold water for 8 hours or longer. Drain and discard the soaking water. Rinse under cold water and drain again. Combine the beans with 6 cups cold water in a medium saucepan over medium-high heat. When the water begins to boil, lower the heat and simmer, uncovered, about 1 hour, until the beans are tender. Season with salt, turn off the heat, and allow to cool to room temperature. Drain.

Drop the garlic into a food processor or blender while it is running to finely chop it. Add the drained, cooked beans to the container with the lemon juice and process about 1 minute to puree the beans. Scrape down the sides of the work bowl. With the machine running, add the olive oil in a steady stream. Stop the machine and scrape the sides down one or two times, until the contents are smooth. Season with salt and pepper to taste. Turn the machine on and off a few times to combine the salt and pepper into the bean spread.

Serve at room temperature, with a drizzle of olive oil over the top and the bread on the side.

MAKES 6 SERVINGS

TOASTED BREAD WITH WHITE BEANS AND TOMATO

A sumptuous appetizer of beans and tomatoes served on thick slices of lightly toasted country-style bread. If you can find it, I recommend Tuscan bread, which is unsalted. It may be hard to come by, unless you bake your own. Other types of country loaves make good substitutes.

Cut the slices about 1 inch thick and lightly toast them. You and your guests can eat the bruschetta with a knife and fork, but fingers are much more fun.

1	CUP DRIED CANNELLINI OR GREAT NORTHERN BEANS OR 2 CUPS COOKED WHITE BEANS, DRAINED
	SALT
2	TABLESPOONS OLIVE OIL
2	LARGE CLOVES GARLIC, 1 FINELY CHOPPED, 1 WHOLE
	PINCH OF PEPERONCINO (RED PEPPER FLAKES)
1	MEDIUM RED ONION, FINELY CHOPPED
1	MEDIUM RIPE TOMATO, CORED, SEEDED, AND CHOPPED
4	SLICES (1 INCH THICK) TUSCAN OR OTHER COUNTRY-STYLE BREAD
	EXTRA VIRGIN OLIVE OIL, FOR SERVING
5	STEMS FRESH ITALIAN FLAT-LEAF PARSLEY, LEAVES ONLY, CHOPPED

If you are using dried beans, soak them in cold water for 8 hours or longer. Drain and discard the soaking water. Rinse under cold water and drain again. Combine the beans with 6 cups cold water in a medium saucepan over medium-high heat. When the water begins to boil, lower the heat and simmer, uncovered, about 1 hour, until the beans are tender. Season with salt, turn off the heat, and allow to cool to room temperature. Drain.

Heat the olive oil in a medium skillet over medium heat. Add the chopped garlic, peperoncino, and onion and cook, stirring, 5 to 7 minutes, until the onion has softened but isn't brown. Stir in the tomato and continue cooking until it begins to give up its juice and lose its bright red color, 2 to 3 minutes longer. Add the cooked beans and season with salt to taste. Using a wooden spoon, stir the beans into the onion and tomato mixture while mashing the beans against the side of the skillet. Continue cooking and stirring until the mixture is heated through and about half the beans remain whole. Turn off the heat and set aside.

While the beans are cooking, toast the bread until lightly browned on the edges (you don't want it to be well-browned). Place the toast on a serving plate and rub the whole clove of garlic over the surface of the toast to lightly flavor it. Drizzle extra virgin olive oil over the toast slices. Spoon some of the bean and tomato mixture onto each piece of toast and sprinkle parsley over the beans.

MAKES **4** SERVINGS

WHIPPED CHICKPEA AND POTATO SPREAD FOR CROSTINI

Chickpeas and potatoes are whipped into a rich, flavorful spread. Serve this as a first course with slices of lightly toasted bread. Drizzle extra virgin olive oil over each serving and serve with chopped red onion.

1	CUP CHICKPEAS
2	LEAVES FRESH SAGE
1	BAY LEAF
1	LARGE CLOVE GARLIC, PEELED
1	SMALL POTATO (ABOUT ¼ POUND), PREFERABLY YUKON GOLD OR YELLOW FINN, PEELED AND QUARTERED
1	MEDIUM RED ONION, FINELY CHOPPED
	SALT AND FRESHLY GROUND BLACK PEPPER
¼	CUP EXTRA VIRGIN OLIVE OIL, PLUS MORE FOR SERVING
1	LOAF CRUSTY BREAD, CUT INTO SERVING-SIZE SLICES

Soak the chickpeas in cold water for 8 hours or longer. Drain and discard the soaking water. Rinse under cold water and drain again. Combine with the sage, bay leaf, and garlic in a medium saucepan with 6 cups cold water, and place over medium-high heat. When the water begins to boil, lower the heat and simmer, uncovered, about 1 hour, until the chickpeas are tender. Add the potato and continue cooking 10 to 15 minutes longer, until the potato is tender when pierced with a sharp knife. Drain everything and allow to cool for 30 minutes. Discard the sage and bay leaf.

Combine the chickpeas and potato with 1 heaping tablespoon of the onion in a food processor. Process to combine the ingredients. With the machine running, add the olive oil and continue processing until the contents are lightly whipped and smooth. Add salt and pepper to taste and process to combine.

Toast the bread until lightly browned.

Serve the spread on individual serving plates with a heaping spoonful of chopped onion, a drizzle of olive oil, and the toast on the side.

MAKES 4 SERVINGS

LENTIL SPREAD FOR CROSTINI

Reminiscent of a fine pâté, this spread is perfect with a glass of wine before dinner.

⅔ CUP ITALIAN SMALL BROWN LENTILS OR FRENCH GREEN LENTILS

1 SMALL CARROT, FINELY CHOPPED

1 SMALL ONION, FINELY CHOPPED

½ RIB CELERY, FINELY CHOPPED

2 CLOVES GARLIC, PEELED

3 TABLESPOONS OLIVE OIL

3 SMALL LEAVES FRESH SAGE

SALT AND FRESHLY GROUND BLACK PEPPER

1 LOAF FRENCH BREAD, THINLY SLICED

EXTRA VIRGIN OLIVE OIL, FOR SERVING

5 STEMS FRESH ITALIAN FLAT-LEAF PARSLEY, LEAVES ONLY, FINELY CHOPPED

Combine the lentils, carrot, onion, celery, 1 clove garlic, 1 tablespoon olive oil, and sage in a saucepan with 4 cups cold water. Bring to a boil, lower the heat, and simmer, uncovered, 30 to 45 minutes, until the lentils are tender.

Drain the lentils and transfer to a food processor or blender. Add the remaining clove of garlic and process until smooth. Season with salt and pepper, add the remaining 2 tablespoons olive oil, and process to combine. Transfer to a container, cover, and refrigerate at least 4 hours before serving.

Toast the bread until it is lightly browned.

Spoon some of the lentil mixture onto the toast, drizzle with olive oil, and sprinkle with parsley.

MAKES 6 SERVINGS

Crostini di fave con la buccia

WHOLE FAVA BEAN SPREAD FOR CROSTINI

A specialty of the area around the southeastern Italian city of Foggia, this coarse, rustic spread has the fava bean skins chopped and blended into it.

1	CUP DRIED WHOLE FAVA BEANS
½	CUP OLIVE OIL, PLUS MORE FOR SERVING
2	CLOVES GARLIC, PEELED
	SALT AND FRESHLY GROUND BLACK PEPPER
	DRIED OREGANO LEAVES
1	SMALL LOAF FRENCH OR RUSTIC COUNTRY BREAD, THINLY SLICED

Soak the beans in cold water for 8 hours or overnight. Drain and discard the soaking water. Rinse under cold water and drain again. Trim the ends of the beans to remove the black seed in the beans' tips. Put the beans in a medium saucepan with 1 tablespoon of the olive oil, 1 clove of the garlic, and 6 cups cold water. Place over medium-high heat and bring the water to a boil. Lower the heat and simmer, uncovered, 1 to 1½ hours, until the beans are tender.

Drain the beans and transfer to a food processor or blender. Add the remaining garlic, 7 tablespoons olive oil, and salt and pepper to taste. Turn the machine on and off to chop the beans. The spread should be chunky. Transfer to a small, shallow serving dish. Drizzle olive oil over the spread and sprinkle with the oregano to cover.

Toast the bread until lightly browned. Serve with the spread.

MAKES 6 SERVINGS

Crostini di fave bianche

FAVA BEAN SPREAD

When fava beans are skinned and dried, they're whitish yellow and called fave bianche. *These make an altogether different, creamy-smooth spread than the one in the previous recipe. The skinned favas require no soaking and only 30 to 45 minutes of cooking. Drain them well, as they tend to absorb a lot of water during cooking.*

1	CUP DRIED SPLIT, SKINNED FAVA BEANS
2	BAY LEAVES
1	LARGE CLOVE GARLIC, PEELED AND CHOPPED
⅓	CUP OLIVE OIL, PLUS MORE FOR SERVING
	SALT AND FRESHLY GROUND BLACK PEPPER
1	SMALL LOAF FRENCH OR RUSTIC COUNTRY BREAD, THINLY SLICED

Combine the fava beans with the bay leaves and 4 to 6 cups cold water in a medium saucepan. Place over medium-high heat and bring the water to a boil. Lower the heat and simmer, uncovered, about 30 minutes, until the beans are tender and can be broken apart with a wooden spoon. Drain and discard the cooking water. Discard the bay leaves.

Transfer the favas to a food processor or blender. Add the garlic and process until the mixture is chopped. Scrape down the sides of the container. With the machine running, add the olive oil in a steady stream. Add salt and pepper to taste and process to incorporate. Transfer to a shallow serving dish. Drizzle olive oil over the spread before serving.

Toast the bread until lightly browned. Serve with the spread.

MAKES 6 SERVINGS

Fave arrostite

ROASTED FAVA BEANS

Fave arrostite, *roasted favas, are also called* fave delle monache, *literally "nun's favas," because when roasted with their skins, favas have the appearance of a nun in her wimple. They are a deliciously crunchy snack. Bianca Tragni, a professor of Pugliese culture at the university in Altamura, gave me this recipe. She said it's traditional to make roasted fava beans for the festival of San Giuseppe, when many bean dishes are prepared. And families in Puglia often have roasted favas on the table on Sundays for the children to nibble while the biggest meal of the week is prepared. In some food shops in Puglia, roasted favas are sold ready to eat.*

1   CUP DRIED WHOLE FAVA BEANS
1   TEASPOON OLIVE OIL
    SALT

Soak the beans in cold water for 8 hours or overnight. Drain and discard the soaking water. Rinse under cold water and drain again. Trim the ends of the beans to remove the black seed in the beans' tips.

Preheat the oven to 400 degrees.

Place the beans in a single layer on a baking sheet. Bake 50 minutes to 1 hour, until the beans become dark brown. Remove the beans from the oven, place them in a serving bowl, and, while still hot, mix with the olive oil and salt to taste. Cool before serving.

MAKES 4 SERVINGS

CHICKPEA CRÊPE

A typical Ligurian snack and street food that's consumed from late morning until late evening, farinata is a wonderful appetizer to serve before dinner with a glass of cold white wine. Although it's prepared throughout Liguria, farinata connoisseurs say it's best along the coast south of Genoa. I learned how to prepare farinata watching the cook at the Osteria Luchin in Chiavari. He filled his very large, round, shallow steel pan with the thin batter—made only of chickpea flour, water, and olive oil—and baked the farinata in a wood-burning oven. The finished crêpe is crispy, lightly browned, deliciously salty, and just a little bit oily—in the way the best snacks are. The top is always heavily dusted with freshly ground black pepper. You can make a very good version in a conventional home oven with a large cast-iron skillet or pizza pan.

1½	CUPS CHICKPEA FLOUR (SEE INGREDIENT GUIDE ON PAGE 19)
2	CUPS COLD WATER
6	TABLESPOONS OLIVE OIL
1	TABLESPOON SALT
	FRESHLY GROUND BLACK PEPPER

Prepare the batter 4 to 8 hours before you want to serve the farinata. Combine the chickpea flour and water in a large mixing bowl and stir vigorously with a wire whisk until the batter is smooth and any lumps of flour are gone. Stir in 2 tablespoons olive oil and the salt. Cover with plastic wrap and allow to stand at room temperature until ready to cook.

Preheat the oven to 550 degrees.

Pour the remaining 4 tablespoons olive oil into a well-seasoned 12- or 14-inch round cast-iron skillet. Add the batter and stir to combine with the olive oil. Place on the top shelf in the oven and bake 15 to 20 minutes, until the edges are brown and the top is just beginning to brown. Season generously with black pepper. Cut into serving pieces.

MAKES 6 TO 8 SERVINGS (1 CRÊPE)

WHITE BEAN AND ONION FRITTERS

Traditionally, frittelle *are sweet or savory foods that are coated with batter and deep fried. They are common throughout Italy. A mixture of cannelli and sauteed red onion, these small, crispy* frittelle *from Liguria are unconventional, but they couldn't be easier or more delectable.*

1 CUP DRIED CANNELLINI OR GREAT NORTHERN BEANS OR 2 CUPS COOKED WHITE BEANS, DRAINED
SALT

2 TABLESPOONS OLIVE OIL, PLUS MORE FOR COOKING

1 MEDIUM RED ONION, FINELY CHOPPED
FRESHLY GROUND BLACK PEPPER

2 TABLESPOONS PLUS ½ CUP UNBLEACHED WHITE FLOUR

If you are using dried beans, soak them in cold water for 8 hours or longer. Drain and discard the soaking water. Rinse under cold water and drain again. Combine the beans with 6 cups cold water in a medium saucepan over medium-high heat. When the water begins to boil, lower the heat and simmer, uncovered, about 1 hour, until the beans are tender. Season with salt, turn off the heat, and allow to cool to room temperature. Drain.

Pass the beans through a food mill or puree in a blender or food processor. Place the pureed beans in a medium mixing bowl and set aside.

Heat 2 tablespoons olive oil in a medium skillet over medium heat. Add the onion and cook, stirring frequently, 7 to 10 minutes, until translucent. Add the cooked onion to the beans. Season with salt and pepper to taste. Add 2 tablespoons flour and with a wooden spoon, stir to combine the ingredients. Wipe the skillet with a paper towel.

Using your hands, form small balls of the bean and onion mixture, about the size of a golf ball. Flatten into ¼-inch-thick rounds, 2 to 3 inches in diameter. Lightly coat with flour.

Heat enough olive oil to barely coat the bottom of the skillet. When the oil is hot but not smoking, add 3 or 4 frittelle to the pan, being careful they are not touching. Cook 5 to 7 minutes on each side, until crisp and golden brown. Drain briefly on paper towels. Repeat to make the remaining frittelle.

MAKES 4 SERVINGS (8 FRITTELLE)

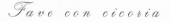

FAVA BEANS WITH CHICORY

This is a traditional recipe from Puglia. Also called fave 'ncapriata *in Pugliese dialect, it is a staple of the cuisine there. You will find some variation of it on nearly every menu, and most households prepare it every week. The rustic, not quite smooth puree of mashed favas, seasoned only with salt, is served alongside boiled greens, usually wild chicory (what we think of as dandelion greens). The two are doused with olive oil and mixed together on the plate. The long strands of the chicory are twirled on the fork like spaghetti, and the fava puree is like a sauce. If you don't have* chicory, you can use other cooked greens such as kale, chard, or broccoli rabe, but the distinctive flavor of this dish comes from the bitterness of both the favas and the greens. I learned the subtleties of cooking this dish from Concetta LaGrua, a wonderful cook in Lecce in southern Puglia. This is usually served as a first course.

1	CUP DRIED SPLIT, SKINNED FAVA BEANS
	SALT
1	POUND CHICORY OR DANDELION GREENS, BOTTOM ENDS TRIMMED, RINSED UNDER COLD WATER
3	TABLESPOONS OLIVE OIL

Put the favas in a medium saucepan with enough cold water to reach about 2 inches above the beans. Place over medium-high heat and bring the water to a boil. Lower the heat and simmer, stirring occasionally, about 45 minutes. After 45 minutes, begin to stir more frequently. As the water cooks away, the beans will become tender and form a semismooth puree, like mashed potatoes. When the beans are finished, stir in the salt, cover, and set aside.

Meanwhile, bring a large pot of water to a boil over high heat. Add 1 tablespoon salt and the chicory and cook, stirring occasionally, 15 minutes. Drain in a colander and season with salt to taste. To serve, place a heaping spoonful of the fava bean puree on one side of a plate. Alongside it, place some of the greens. Dress with olive oil.

MAKES 6 SERVINGS

Fagioli alla maruzzara

WHITE BEANS WITH TOMATOES AND BREAD

A specialty from the town of San Giovanni near Naples, this stew of white beans and tomatoes is served over slices of bread. The traditional bread of San Giovanni, hefty 5-pound loaves, is still baked in wood-burning ovens.

1	CUP DRIED CANNELLINI OR GREAT NORTHERN BEANS
2	BAY LEAVES
¼	CUP OLIVE OIL
1	RIB CELERY, FINELY CHOPPED
1	LARGE CLOVE GARLIC, PEELED AND FINELY CHOPPED
2	CUPS CANNED WHOLE PEELED TOMATOES, DRAINED AND COARSELY CHOPPED
15	STEMS FRESH ITALIAN FLAT-LEAF PARSLEY, LEAVES ONLY, CHOPPED
1	TEASPOON DRIED OREGANO
	SALT AND FRESHLY GROUND BLACK PEPPER
4	SLICES (1 INCH EACH) RUSTIC COUNTRY BREAD

Soak the beans in cold water for 8 hours or longer. Drain and discard the soaking water. Rinse under cold water and drain again. Combine the beans with the bay leaves and 6 cups cold water in a medium saucepan over medium-high heat. When the water begins to boil, lower the heat and simmer, uncovered, about 1 hour, until the beans are tender. Drain and discard the bay leaves.

Heat the olive oil in a medium skillet over medium heat. Add the celery and garlic and cook, stirring, about 1 minute, until the celery begins to soften. Be careful not to brown the garlic. Add the tomatoes, parsley, and oregano and cook, stirring, 5 minutes. Add the beans, season with salt and pepper to taste, and continue cooking about 15 minutes longer.

Meanwhile, lightly toast the bread and arrange the slices on individual serving plates. Spoon the beans over each piece of toast and serve.

MAKES 4 SERVINGS

Sformatini di fagioli bianchi e bietole

TIMBALES OF WHITE BEANS AND SWISS CHARD

Sformatini *are small soufflés or custards, and they are typical Tuscan antipasti. You can substitute spinach for the chard.*

SFORMATINI
½   CUP DRIED CANNELLINI OR GREAT NORTHERN BEANS OR 1 CUP COOKED WHITE BEANS, DRAINED

3   LARGE LEAVES FRESH SAGE

1   LARGE CLOVE GARLIC, PEELED
SALT

1   BUNCH GREEN SWISS CHARD, RINSED, STEMMED, AND COARSELY CHOPPED

2   WHOLE EGGS

2   TABLESPOONS FRESHLY GRATED PARMIGIANO CHEESE

¼   CUP MASCARPONE CHEESE (SEE INGREDIENT GUIDE ON PAGE 19)
FRESHLY GROUND BLACK PEPPER

TOMATO SAUCE
¼   CUP OLIVE OIL

1   LARGE CLOVE GARLIC, PEELED AND FINELY CHOPPED

1   CUP CHOPPED FRESH OR CANNED PEELED TOMATOES
SALT AND FRESHLY GROUND BLACK PEPPER

8   LEAVES FRESH BASIL

To prepare the sformatini: Soak the beans in cold water for 8 hours or longer. Drain and discard the soaking water. Combine the beans with the sage and garlic and 4 cups cold water in a medium saucepan over medium-high heat. When the water begins to boil, lower the heat and simmer, uncovered, about 1 hour, until the beans are tender. Remove and discard the sage and garlic, season with salt, turn off the heat, and allow to cool to room temperature.

Bring a large pot of water to a boil over high heat. Add the chard and cook, stirring occasionally, for 15 minutes. Drain in a colander and rinse under cold water. When the chard is cool enough to handle, take handfuls and gently squeeze the water from it.

Drain the beans and combine with the chard, eggs, parmigiano, and mascarpone in a food processor or blender. Season with salt and pepper to taste. Process about 1 minute, until the mixture is smooth. Scrape the sides down with a rubber spatula. Continue processing about 1 minute longer.

Preheat the oven to 350 degrees.

Spoon about ½ cup of the bean mixture into 4 buttered 1-cup glass or porcelain ramekins, to fill them two-thirds full. Place the ramekins in a shallow baking pan and add enough hot water to the pan to reach three-quarters of the way up the sides of the ramekins.

Bake 35 to 40 minutes, until the sformatini are firm and set and a sharp knife inserted into one comes out clean. Allow the ramekins to cool 2 to 3 minutes before unmolding.

To prepare the tomato sauce: While the sformatini are cooking, heat the olive oil in a medium saucepan over medium heat. Add the garlic and cook about 1 minute, being careful not to brown it. Add the tomatoes, season with salt and pepper to taste, and simmer gently, stirring frequently, about 20 minutes, until the sauce has thickened. Tear the basil leaves into small pieces and add to the tomato sauce. Stir well to combine. Turn off the heat and set aside. Reheat before serving.

Unmold the sformatini on individual plates and serve with fresh tomato sauce on the side.

MAKES 4 SERVINGS

Insalata di fagioli con alici e erbe

BEAN SALAD WITH ANCHOVIES AND HERBS

This tangy salad is from the Veneto, where sweet-and-sour flavorings are traditional and borlotti are the favorite beans. The combination of red wine vinegar and anchovies makes this a highly seasoned and flavorful first course. Serve over lightly dressed greens, with some good crusty bread.

1	CUP DRIED BORLOTTI, PINTO, OR CRANBERRY BEANS
¼	CUP EXTRA VIRGIN OLIVE OIL
1	CLOVE GARLIC, PEELED
3	ANCHOVIES PACKED IN SALT, RINSED IN COLD WATER, FILLETED, AND CHOPPED, OR 6 ANCHOVY FILLETS PACKED IN OIL, DRAINED AND CHOPPED (SEE INGREDIENT GUIDE ON PAGE 19)
15	STEMS FRESH ITALIAN FLAT-LEAF PARSLEY, LEAVES ONLY, CHOPPED
2	TABLESPOONS RED WINE VINEGAR
	SALT AND FRESHLY GROUND BLACK PEPPER

Soak the beans in cold water for 8 hours or longer. Drain and discard the soaking water. Rinse under cold water and drain again. Combine the beans with 6 cups cold water in a medium saucepan over medium-high heat. When the water begins to boil, lower the heat and simmer, uncovered, 1 to 1½ hours, until the beans are tender. Turn off the heat and set aside.

Heat the olive oil in a medium saucepan over medium heat. Add the garlic and cook about 5 minutes, just until it begins to turn brown. Add the anchovies and use a wooden spoon to mash them into the oil. They should dissolve quickly. Stir in the parsley and vinegar and continue cooking about 5 minutes longer. Drain the beans and add to the anchovy sauce. Season cautiously, because the anchovies are salty, with salt and pepper to taste and mix well. Serve at room temperature.

MAKES 4 SERVINGS

Insalata di lenticchie

LENTIL SALAD

This is a versatile salad that can be an appetizer or a savory light luncheon main course. Small lentils tend to keep their shape and hold up to cooking, which is essential for this salad.

2 CUPS ITALIAN SMALL BROWN LENTILS OR FRENCH GREEN LENTILS

1 MEDIUM RED ONION, PEELED AND SOAKED IN COLD WATER FOR 30 MINUTES, FINELY CHOPPED

¼ CUP EXTRA VIRGIN OLIVE OIL

2 TABLESPOONS RED WINE VINEGAR

SALT AND FRESHLY GROUND BLACK PEPPER

15 STEMS FRESH ITALIAN FLAT-LEAF PARSLEY, LEAVES ONLY, CHOPPED

6 CUPS SALAD GREENS, SUCH AS MESCLUN, LETTUCE, OR ARUGULA, OR A COMBINATION

1 TABLESPOON OLIVE OIL

Combine the lentils with 6 cups cold water in a medium saucepan and place over high heat. When the water begins to boil, lower the heat and simmer, uncovered, 30 to 45 minutes, until the lentils are tender. Drain in a strainer and rinse well under cold water.

Allow the lentils to cool to room temperature. Add the onion, extra virgin olive oil, vinegar, and salt and pepper to taste. Stir in the parsley until combined.

Season the salad greens with salt and pepper to taste, toss with the olive oil, and arrange on a platter. Spoon the lentils onto the bed of greens and serve.

MAKES 4 SERVINGS

Insalata di lenticchie e formaggio

SALAD OF LENTILS AND CHEESE

This salad from Citta di Castello in Umbria makes a perfect first course. Use Italian brown lentils or green French lentils—they keep their shape and firmness even when cooked.

1   CUP ITALIAN SMALL BROWN LENTILS OR FRENCH GREEN LENTILS

1   CLOVE GARLIC, PEELED

2   LEAVES FRESH SAGE

    SALT AND FRESHLY GROUND BLACK PEPPER

1   MEDIUM RIPE TOMATO, CORED, SEEDED, AND COARSELY CHOPPED

¼   CUP OLIVE OIL, PLUS MORE FOR SERVING

⅓   CUP GRATED GRANA OR PARMIGIANO CHEESE

8   STEMS FRESH ITALIAN FLAT-LEAF PARSLEY, LEAVES ONLY, CHOPPED

Put the lentils in a medium saucepan with the garlic, sage, and 6 cups cold water and place over medium-high heat. When the water begins to boil, lower the heat and simmer, uncovered, 30 to 45 minutes, until the lentils are tender. Drain in a strainer. Discard the garlic and sage.

Transfer the lentils to a mixing bowl. Season with salt and pepper to taste. Stir in the tomato, olive oil, and cheese and mix well. Garnish each serving with a drizzle of olive oil and chopped parsley.

MAKES 4 SERVINGS

SALAD OF CORONA BEANS

Coronas *are the biggest beans encountered in Italy. They're shaped like lima beans, but they're almost 2 inches long when dried and swell up to be even bigger once they're cooked. Coronas are found all over Italy and are almost always served in a salad. A comparable bean is the Greek gigante bean, which can be found in Middle Eastern markets. I sampled this salad at a remarkable food shop in Rome called Franchi, which offers an expansive and elegant selection of prepared foods. You can easily prepare this dish with any white beans.*

1	CUP DRIED CORONA OR CANNELLINI BEANS OR 2 CUPS COOKED WHITE BEANS, DRAINED
1	CLOVE GARLIC, PEELED
2	BAY LEAVES
	SALT
2	RIBS CELERY, CHOPPED
1	MEDIUM CARROT, GRATED
1	MEDIUM RED ONION, CHOPPED
5	STEMS FRESH ITALIAN FLAT-LEAF PARSLEY, LEAVES ONLY, CHOPPED
	FRESHLY GROUND BLACK PEPPER
¼	CUP OLIVE OIL

If you are using dried beans, soak them in cold water for 8 hours or longer. Drain and discard the soaking water. Rinse under cold water and drain again. Combine the beans with the garlic, bay leaves, and 6 cups cold water in a medium saucepan over medium-high heat. When the water begins to boil, lower the heat and simmer, uncovered, about 1 hour, until the beans are tender. Season with salt and allow to cool to room temperature. Drain and discard the garlic and bay leaves.

Combine the cooked beans with the celery, carrot, onion, and parsley in a large mixing bowl. Add salt and pepper to taste and the olive oil. Stir well to combine and let stand about 15 minutes to allow the flavors to blend.

MAKES 4 SERVINGS

Insalata lessa

SALAD OF WHITE BEANS AND TUNA

A wonderful dish to serve any time of year, this salad is prepared in many parts of Italy. I rarely eat it there because it is one of my family's favorite dishes, and it's a Saturday staple at home. I made it for years with my sandwich tuna (white, packed in water) until a friend suggested I use Italian tuna packed in olive oil, the kind they use in Italy. The change was a revelation. Italian tuna has so much more flavor than its comparatively bland American counterpart that I won't even prepare this salad now unless I have Italian tuna on hand. This dish is traditionally made with red onions. I like to prepare it with scallions for a different but delicious taste.

1   CUP DRIED CANNELLINI OR GREAT NORTHERN BEANS OR 2 CUPS COOKED WHITE BEANS, DRAINED

    SALT

1   6- OR 7-OUNCE CAN TUNA PACKED IN OLIVE OIL (SEE INGREDIENT GUIDE ON PAGE 19), NOT DRAINED

1   MEDIUM RED ONION, PEELED AND SOAKED IN COLD WATER FOR 30 MINUTES, FINELY CHOPPED, OR 4 SCALLIONS, ROOTS TRIMMED, THINLY SLICED

¼   CUP EXTRA VIRGIN OLIVE OIL

    FRESHLY GROUND BLACK PEPPER

If you are using dried beans, soak them in cold water for 8 hours or longer. Drain and discard the soaking water. Rinse under cold water and drain again. Combine the beans with 6 cups cold water in a medium saucepan over medium-high heat. When the water begins to boil, lower the heat and simmer, uncovered, about 1 hour, until the beans are tender. Season with salt, turn off the heat, and allow to cool to room temperature. Drain.

Transfer the beans to a medium mixing bowl. Flake the tuna with a fork and add it, along with the oil it's packed in, to the beans with the onion or scallions. Add the olive oil, season with salt and pepper to taste, and mix well to combine. Serve at room temperature.

MAKES 4 SERVINGS

Insalata di fagioli e bottarga

SALAD OF WHITE BEANS AND BOTTARGA

Bottarga *is the preserved roe from tuna or mullet. It is taken from the fish as soon as the fish is caught, then salted, pressed into a small, brick-shaped cake, and smoked. A delicacy that is always served very thinly sliced or even grated, it can be marinated in lemon juice and olive oil as part of an antipasto, tossed with pasta, or combined with white beans as in this recipe. I first tasted this dish in Venice at a restaurant called Da Ivo, which overlooks a small canal where you can watch the gondoliers rowing by as you enjoy your meal.*

1½ CUPS DRIED CANNELLINI OR GREAT NORTHERN BEANS OR 3 CUPS COOKED WHITE BEANS, DRAINED
SALT

¼ CUP OLIVE OIL, OR MORE TO TASTE
JUICE OF 1 LEMON
FRESHLY GROUND BLACK PEPPER

15 STEMS FRESH ITALIAN FLAT-LEAF PARSLEY, LEAVES ONLY, CHOPPED

2 OUNCES BOTTARGA (SEE INGREDIENT GUIDE ON PAGE 19), PEELED AND VERY THINLY SLICED OR SHAVED WITH A VEGETABLE PEELER

If you are using dried beans, soak them in cold water for 8 hours or longer. Drain and discard the soaking water. Rinse under cold water and drain again. Combine the beans with 6 cups cold water in a medium saucepan over medium-high heat. When the water begins to boil, lower the heat and simmer, uncovered, about 1 hour, until the beans are tender.

Season with salt, turn off the heat, and allow to cool to room temperature. Drain.

Combine the cooked beans with the olive oil, lemon juice, salt and pepper to taste, and parsley in a medium mixing bowl. Mix well. Divide the beans equally among individual serving plates. Top each serving with some of the sliced bottarga.

MAKES 4 SERVINGS

SALAD OF WHITE BEANS, SHRIMP, AND TOMATO

White beans and shrimp are a favorite antipasto throughout Tuscany. I like to prepare this dish with small white Tuscan zolfino or soranini beans. A good substitute is Great Northern. When they're in season, I use small fresh rock shrimp to prepare this dish. Serve warm or at room temperature, either as a first course or as a deliciously light entree.

1	CUP DRIED SMALL WHITE BEANS, SUCH AS ZOLFINO, SORANINI, GREAT NORTHERN, OR NAVY, OR 2 CUPS COOKED WHITE BEANS, DRAINED
2	LARGE CLOVES GARLIC, PEELED, 1 WHOLE, 1 FINELY CHOPPED
1	LEAF FRESH SAGE
	SALT
1	POUND FRESH SMALL SHRIMP, PEELED AND DEVEINED
2	MEDIUM RIPE TOMATOES, CORED, SEEDED, AND FINELY DICED
8	LARGE LEAVES FRESH BASIL, SHREDDED
	FRESHLY GROUND BLACK PEPPER
1/3	CUP OLIVE OIL

If you are using dried beans, soak them in cold water for 8 hours or longer. Drain and discard the soaking water. Rinse under cold water and drain again. Combine the beans with the whole clove of garlic, sage, and 6 cups cold water in a medium saucepan over medium-high heat. When the water begins to boil, lower the heat and simmer, uncovered, about 1 hour, until the beans are tender. Season with salt, turn off the heat, and allow to cool to room temperature. Drain and discard the garlic and sage.

Bring a small saucepan of water to a boil. Add the shrimp and cook 1 minute, or just until the shrimp turn bright pink. Drain and set aside.

In a large mixing bowl, combine the shrimp with the cooked beans, tomatoes, basil, and salt and pepper to taste. Add the olive oil and mix well. Serve at room temperature.

MAKES 4 SERVINGS

WARM SALAD OF OCTOPUS AND WHITE BEANS

Octopus and beans are commonly paired in Tuscany, particularly along the coast, where all manner of seafood is combined with white beans. Octopus is not as daunting as it may seem. I have only cooked with fresh octopus (many cooks use the frozen variety without hesitation), which requires some cleaning and cutting, but simple boiling will render it as tender as you could possibly want. This salad should be served warm, so cook the octopus just before you plan to serve it.

½ CUP DRIED SMALL WHITE BEANS, SUCH AS SORANINI, TOSCANELLO, GREAT NORTHERN, OR NAVY, OR 1 CUP COOKED WHITE BEANS, DRAINED

4 LARGE LEAVES FRESH SAGE

SALT

1 POUND FRESH OCTOPUS, TENTACLES CUT INTO INDIVIDUAL PIECES, HEAD TRIMMED FROM THE INNER PARTS AND CUT INTO BITE-SIZE PIECES

1 TABLESPOON FRESH LEMON JUICE, OR MORE TO TASTE

¼ CUP OLIVE OIL, PLUS MORE FOR SERVING

FRESHLY GROUND BLACK PEPPER

5 STEMS FRESH ITALIAN FLAT-LEAF PARSLEY, LEAVES ONLY, CHOPPED

If you are using dried beans, soak them in cold water for 8 hours or longer. Drain and discard the soaking water. Rinse under cold water and drain again. Combine the beans with the sage and 4 cups cold water in a medium saucepan over medium-high heat. When the water begins to boil, lower the heat and simmer, uncovered, about 1 hour, until the beans are tender. Season with salt, remove from the heat, and allow to cool to room temperature. Drain and discard the sage leaves.

Clean the octopus and put it in a medium saucepan with 1 tablespoon salt and ample water to cover. Place over medium-high heat. When the water begins to boil, lower the heat, cover the pan, and simmer, about 45 minutes, until the octopus is tender. Drain in a colander.

Combine the cooked beans with the octopus in a medium mixing bowl. Add the lemon juice, olive oil, and salt and pepper to taste.

Serve with a drizzle of olive oil and a pinch of parsley on each serving.

MAKES 4 SERVINGS

Insalata calda di fagioli e calamari al pesto

WARM SALAD OF WHITE BEANS, SQUID, AND PESTO

In Liguria, pesto is a staple of the cuisine. This warm salad of lightly cooked squid, beans, and potatoes is rich and flavorful but still a delicate preparation. The white beans grown in Liguria include fagioli di Pigna, fagioli di Conio, and fagioli di Badalucco. They are rarely available outside of Liguria. Cannellini are a good alternative.

SALAD

1   CUP DRIED FAGIOLI DI PIGNA, CANNELLINI, OR GREAT NORTHERN BEANS, OR 2 CUPS COOKED WHITE BEANS, DRAINED

1   LARGE CLOVE GARLIC, PEELED

3   LEAVES FRESH SAGE

6   TABLESPOONS OLIVE OIL

SALT

1   MEDIUM YUKON GOLD OR YELLOW FINN POTATO, PEELED AND CUT INTO 1-INCH DICE

1   POUND FRESH SQUID, CLEANED AND BODY CUT INTO ¼-INCH SLICES, TENTACLES LEFT WHOLE

FRESHLY GROUND BLACK PEPPER

PESTO

2   CUPS LIGHTLY PACKED FRESH BASIL LEAVES, RINSED IN COLD WATER, DRIED

1   LARGE CLOVE GARLIC, PEELED

2   TABLESPOONS PIGNOLI NUTS (PINE NUTS)

½   CUP OLIVE OIL

SALT

To prepare the salad: If you are using dried beans, soak them in cold water for 8 hours or longer. Drain and discard the soaking water. Combine the beans with the garlic, sage, 2 tablespoons olive oil, and 6 cups cold water in a medium saucepan over medium-high heat. When the water begins to boil, lower the heat and simmer, uncovered, about 1 hour, until the beans are tender. Season with salt, turn off the heat, and allow to cool to room temperature. Drain and discard the garlic and sage. Transfer the beans to a large mixing bowl.

Meanwhile, place the cut potato in a small saucepan with water to cover. Bring the water to a boil, lower the heat, and simmer 10 to 15 minutes, until the potato is tender when pierced with a sharp knife. Drain and add to the beans.

Bring another small saucepan of water to a boil. Add the squid and cook 1 to 2 minutes. Do not overcook or the squid will be tough. Drain and add the squid to the bowl with the beans and potatoes. Add the remaining 4 tablespoons olive oil, season with salt and pepper to taste, and stir well to combine.

To prepare the pesto: Combine the basil, garlic, and pine nuts in a food processor or blender. Process about 1 minute. Scrape down the sides of the container. With the machine running, add the ½ cup olive oil in a steady stream and continue processing until the mixture is smooth. Season with salt to taste and turn the machine on and off to combine.

Divide the bean, potato, and squid mixture among individual serving plates. Garnish each serving with a heaping spoonful of pesto.

MAKES 4 SERVINGS

Insalata di cannellini e frutti di mare

WARM SALAD OF CANNELLINI BEANS AND SEAFOOD

I was served this simple salad of seafood and white beans in Florence at the Cantina Antinori, a beautiful little wine bar in an old palazzo run by the eminent Antinori winery. The key here is ultra-fresh fish and delicately cooked beans. If fresh squid isn't available, substitute more shrimp. I like this recipe because you can stretch it to feed a bigger crowd.

1 CUP DRIED SMALL WHITE BEANS, SUCH AS ZOLFINI, SORANINI, GREAT NORTHERN, OR NAVY, OR 2 CUPS COOKED WHITE BEANS, DRAINED

3 LEAVES FRESH SAGE

SALT

1 POUND FRESH SQUID, CLEANED AND BODIES CUT INTO ¼-INCH SLICES, TENTACLES LEFT WHOLE

½ POUND FRESH SMALL SHRIMP, PEELED AND DEVEINED

1 POUND FRESH MUSSELS IN THEIR SHELLS, RINSED AND CLEANED OF ANY DIRT OR SAND; DISCARD ANY WITH BROKEN SHELLS

FRESHLY GROUND BLACK PEPPER

½ CUP OLIVE OIL

5 STEMS FRESH ITALIAN FLAT-LEAF PARSLEY, LEAVES ONLY, CHOPPED

EXTRA VIRGIN OLIVE OIL, FOR SERVING

If you are using dried beans, soak them in cold water for 8 hours or longer. Drain and discard the soaking water. Rinse under cold water and drain again. Combine the beans with the sage and 6 cups cold water in a medium saucepan over medium-high heat. When the water begins to boil, lower the heat and simmer, uncovered, about 1 hour, until the beans are tender. Season with salt, turn off the heat, and allow to cool to room temperature. Drain and discard the sage.

Bring a small saucepan of water to a boil over medium-high heat. Add the squid and cook for 1 to 2 minutes. Do not overcook or it will become tough. Use a slotted spoon to remove the squid from the water and drain. Transfer to a large mixing bowl. Using the same water, cook the shrimp for 1 to 2 minutes until it turns pink. Drain and add to the mixing bowl with the squid.

Meanwhile, place the mussels in a medium saucepan with ¼ cup water over medium-high heat. Cover and bring to a boil. Lower the heat and cook about 5 minutes, until all the shells are open. Uncover the pot and discard any mussels that did not open. When cool enough to handle, remove the mussels from the opened shells (you should have about ⅓ cup mussels) and combine with the seafood in the mixing bowl.

Add the cooked beans to the bowl with the seafood. Season with salt and pepper to taste, add the olive oil and parsley, and mix well. Serve with a drizzle of extra virgin olive oil on each serving.

MAKES 4 SERVINGS

SALAD OF CHICKPEAS AND SQUID

I enjoyed this salad at a restaurant in Fiumicino, a small city near the Rome airport, where I was staying before a flight home. It makes a perfect appetizer or a wonderful summer main course. Use only the freshest squid, not frozen.

1	CUP DRIED CHICKPEAS OR 2 CUPS COOKED CHICKPEAS, DRAINED
2	BAY LEAVES
	SALT
	JUICE OF ½ LEMON
8	STEMS FRESH ITALIAN FLAT-LEAF PARSLEY, LEAVES ONLY, CHOPPED
1	SMALL CLOVE GARLIC, PEELED AND FINELY CHOPPED
	PINCH OF PEPERONCINO (RED PEPPER FLAKES), OR MORE TO TASTE
¼	CUP EXTRA VIRGIN OLIVE OIL
1	POUND FRESH SQUID, CLEANED AND BODIES CUT INTO ¼-INCH SLICES, TENTACLES LEFT WHOLE
	FRESHLY GROUND BLACK PEPPER

If you are using dried chickpeas, soak them in cold water for 8 hours or longer. Drain and discard the soaking water. Rinse under cold water and drain again. Combine the chickpeas with the bay leaves and 6 cups cold water in a medium saucepan over medium-high heat. When the water begins to boil, lower the heat and simmer, uncovered, about 1 hour, until the beans are tender. Season with salt, remove from the heat, and allow to cool to room temperature. Drain and discard the bay leaves.

Combine the lemon juice, parsley, garlic, peperon-cino, and olive oil in a medium-size mixing bowl. Set aside.

Meanwhile, fill a medium saucepan with cold water and place over high heat. When the water begins to boil, add the squid and cook 1 to 2 minutes. Do not overcook or the squid will become tough. Drain. Add to the bowl with the lemon and oil mixture. Add the cooked beans and stir to combine. Season with salt and pepper to taste. Serve at room temperature.

MAKES 4 SERVINGS

Fagioli di lamon con cipolla

LAMON BEAN SALAD WITH ONIONS

Lamon is a small town in the foothills of the Italian Alps, about an hour north of Venice. The beans they grow there, fagioli di Lamon, *are large, speckled, and dark-skinned. These beans are the lifeblood of this small town. A three-day festival every September there marks the bean harvest, and people come from all over to taste these meaty beans when they're fresh. This salad is one of the traditional preparations there (the others are soups), and it couldn't be more simple. Fagioli di Lamon are not widely available in the United States, so you can use borlotti, cranberry, or pinto beans.*

1   CUP DRIED FAGIOLI DI LAMON, BORLOTTI, CRANBERRY, OR PINTO BEANS

2   SMALL RED ONIONS, 1 PEELED AND LEFT WHOLE, 1 HALVED THROUGH THE ROOT END AND VERY THINLY SLICED

1   SMALL CARROT

1   RIB CELERY, PREFERABLY WITH ITS LEAVES

SALT

¼   CUP EXTRA VIRGIN OLIVE OIL, PLUS MORE FOR SERVING

1   TEASPOON RED WINE VINEGAR OR BALSAMIC VINEGAR

FRESHLY GROUND BLACK PEPPER

5   STEMS FRESH ITALIAN FLAT-LEAF PARSLEY, LEAVES ONLY, FINELY CHOPPED

Soak the beans in cold water for 8 hours or longer. Drain and discard the soaking water. Rinse under cold water and drain again. Combine the beans with the whole onion, carrot, celery, and 6 cups cold water in a large saucepan over medium-high heat. When the water begins to boil, lower the heat and simmer, uncovered, stirring occasionally, 1 to 1½ hours, until the beans are tender but not falling apart. Season with salt, turn off the heat, and allow the beans to cool to room temperature.

When you are ready to serve the salad, drain the beans and transfer them to a large mixing bowl. Discard the onion, carrot, and celery cooked with the beans. Add the olive oil and vinegar to the beans and mix well. Add salt and pepper to taste. Divide the beans among individual serving bowls. Top each serving with a generous helping of the sliced onion, parsley, and a drizzle of olive oil.

MAKES 4 SERVINGS

SALAD OF ARTICHOKE, BEANS, AND SHRIMP

One of my favorite restaurants in all of Italy is Paolo e Barbara in San Remo. Paolo Masieri has worked in some of the most famous kitchens in France and has made his mark in his native Italy, redefining classic Italian dishes in an elegant, modern style. I was served this delicate salad in the early fall, when the first baby artichokes were available there. I recommend preparing this salad with the smallest artichokes that are available here in the early spring. Like the Italian variety, they have no choke and are the tenderest you'll find. This is very important, since the artichokes are not cooked; they're thinly sliced raw and marinated. You will, however, have to trim the baby artichokes of their tough outer leaves. Paolo favors his local fagioli di Pigna, *a plump white* bean that comes from the hills above San Remo. Cannellini or Great Northern beans are good substitutes.

½ CUP DRIED FAGIOLI DI PIGNA, CANNELLINI, OR GREAT NORTHERN BEANS

SALT

6 SMALL OR BABY ARTICHOKES

⅓ CUP OLIVE OIL

JUICE OF 1 LEMON

1 TABLESPOON CHOPPED FRESH ROSEMARY LEAVES

FRESHLY GROUND BLACK PEPPER

8 MEDIUM SHRIMP, PREFERABLY WITH THE HEADS ON, PEELED AND DEVEINED

Soak the beans in cold water for 8 hours or longer. Drain and discard the soaking water. Rinse under cold water and drain again. Combine the beans with 6 cups cold water in a medium saucepan over medium-high heat. When the water begins to boil, lower the heat and simmer, uncovered, about 1 hour, until the beans are tender. Season with salt, turn off the heat, and allow to cool to room temperature.

Cut the top 1 inch off each artichoke and pull away the leaves until only the yellow leaves remain. Use a sharp paring knife to peel the stem and trim around the base. Cut the peeled artichoke in half and slice, vertically, as thinly as possible. Use a slicing blade on a mandoline, if possible, and transfer the slices to a mixing bowl. Add the olive oil, lemon juice, rosemary, and salt and pepper to taste. Allow the artichokes to marinate at least 1 hour, more if possible. This helps to tenderize them.

Just before you are ready to serve the salad, drain the beans and add them to the artichokes. Bring a small saucepan of water to a boil. Add the shrimp and cook 1 to 2 minutes, until they turn pink. Drain. Arrange the artichoke and bean salad on individual serving plates, and place 2 whole shrimp in the center of each plate.

MAKES 4 SERVINGS

CHICKPEA AND OLIVE SALAD

With its assertive, robust flavors, this salad of chickpeas and olives makes a hearty fall or winter appetizer. Gaeta olives are traditional in this dish, but you can use other firm black olives such as kalamata.

1	CUP DRIED CHICKPEAS OR 2 CUPS COOKED CHICKPEAS, DRAINED
2	BAY LEAVES
	SALT
2	OUNCES PANCETTA (SEE INGREDIENT GUIDE ON PAGE 19), CUT INTO SMALL DICE
5	TABLESPOONS EXTRA VIRGIN OLIVE OIL
1	SMALL RED ONION, FINELY CHOPPED
½	CUP PITTED BLACK OLIVES, GAETA OR KALAMATA, QUARTERED
8	STEMS FRESH ITALIAN FLAT-LEAF PARSLEY, LEAVES ONLY, CHOPPED
	FRESHLY GROUND BLACK PEPPER

If you are using dried chickpeas, soak them in cold water for 8 hours or longer. Drain and discard the soaking water. Rinse under cold water and drain again. Combine the chickpeas with the bay leaves and 6 cups cold water in a medium saucepan over medium-high heat. When the water begins to boil, lower the heat and simmer, uncovered, stirring occasionally, about 1 hour, until the beans are tender. Season with salt, turn off the heat, and allow to cool to room temperature. Drain and discard the bay leaves.

Combine the pancetta with 2 tablespoons olive oil in a small skillet over medium-low heat and cook, stirring frequently, about 10 minutes, until the pancetta is crisp. Turn off the heat and set aside to cool slightly.

Combine the cooked chickpeas with the crisp pancetta, onion, and olives in a mixing bowl. Stir in the remaining 3 tablespoons olive oil, the parsley, and salt and pepper to taste.

MAKES 4 SERVINGS

Insalata di fave fresche e pecorino

SALAD OF FRESH BABY FAVA BEANS AND PECORINO CHEESE

Prepare this irresistibly simple salad when fresh favas are readily available in the early spring. Favas require some patience: First you take the beans from their pods, then you peel the outer skin from each bean. The beans are easy to peel with your fingers, but it's time-consuming. Some good olive oil and a moderately aged pecorino toscano cheese are the only other essential ingredients. Don't confuse tangy pecorino toscano with the more assertive pecorino romano.

2   POUNDS FRESH FAVA BEANS, IN THEIR PODS
¼   CUP EXTRA VIRGIN OLIVE OIL
     SALT AND FRESHLY GROUND BLACK PEPPER
8   OUNCES MILDLY AGED PECORINO TOSCANO CHEESE

Bring a medium saucepan of water to a boil.

Meanwhile, shell the fava beans. Drop the shelled favas into the boiling water and cook exactly 1 minute. Drain and rinse under cold water. Use your hands to peel the skins from each fava bean.

Arrange the beans on individual serving plates. Drizzle some of the olive oil over the beans and season with salt and pepper to taste. Cut the cheese into small pieces or shave it with a vegetable peeler, and divide among the plates.

MAKES 4 SERVINGS

Insalata di ceci e verdure

CHICKPEA SALAD WITH TOMATOES AND PEPPERS

I recommend serving this salad when you prepare it. If it stands, the tomatoes make the salad watery and dilute all the good flavors.

1   CUP DRIED CHICKPEAS OR 2 CUPS COOKED
    CHICKPEAS, DRAINED

2   BAY LEAVES
    SALT

1   BELL PEPPER (ANY COLOR), FINELY CHOPPED

1   MEDIUM TOMATO, CORED, SEEDED, AND CHOPPED

1   MEDIUM RED ONION, FINELY CHOPPED

1   CLOVE GARLIC, PEELED AND FINELY CHOPPED

¼   CUP EXTRA VIRGIN OLIVE OIL

5   STEMS FRESH ITALIAN FLAT-LEAF PARSLEY,
    LEAVES ONLY, CHOPPED

    FRESHLY GROUND BLACK PEPPER

Soak dried chickpeas in cold water for 8 hours. Drain and discard the soaking water. Rinse under cold water and drain again. Combine beans with bay leaves and 6 cups cold water in a saucepan over medium-high heat. When the water begins to boil, lower the heat and simmer, uncovered, about 1 hour, until the beans are tender. Season with salt, turn off heat, and allow beans to cool to room temperature. Drain and discard bay leaves.

In a large mixing bowl, combine the cooked chickpeas with the bell pepper, tomato, onion, garlic, olive oil, parsley, and salt and pepper to taste. Stir to combine. Serve immediately.

MAKES 4 SERVINGS

Fagioli e cotiche

BEANS AND PORK RIND

This is Italy's version of pork and beans, and there are variations from nearly every region. This recipe comes from my friend and fellow cookbook author Franco Romagnoli, a Roman who has been living in the Boston area for many years.

1	CUP DRIED CANNELLINI OR GREAT NORTHERN BEANS
4	OUNCES PORK RIND, PANCETTA, OR PROSCIUTTO (SEE INGREDIENT GUIDE ON PAGE 19), CUT INTO 1-INCH PIECES
3	TABLESPOONS OLIVE OIL
1	CLOVE GARLIC, PEELED AND FINELY CHOPPED
1	SMALL RED ONION, FINELY CHOPPED
5	STEMS FRESH ITALIAN FLAT-LEAF PARSLEY, LEAVES ONLY, CHOPPED
1	CUP CANNED WHOLE PEELED TOMATOES, DRAINED AND COARSELY CHOPPED
	SALT AND FRESHLY GROUND BLACK PEPPER

Soak the beans in cold water for 8 hours or longer. Drain and discard the soaking water. Rinse under cold water and drain again. Combine the beans with the pork rind, pancetta, or prosciutto and 6 cups cold water in a medium saucepan over medium-high heat. When the water begins to boil, lower the heat and simmer, uncovered, about 1 hour, until the beans are tender. Drain and reserve the cooking water.

Heat the olive oil in a heavy 4-quart casserole over medium heat. Add the garlic, onion, and parsley and cook 2 to 3 minutes, until the onion begins to soften, being careful not to brown the garlic. Add the tomatoes, beans, and 3 cups of the cooking water. When the liquid begins to simmer, lower the heat and cook slowly, about 30 minutes. Season with salt and pepper to taste.

MAKES 4 SERVINGS

ROMAN BEANS WITH GUANCIALE

Guanciale, *a purely Roman delicacy, is cured pork fat that's taken from the cheek of the pig. It imparts a distinctive flavor to whatever it's cooked with. In this recipe for roman beans, which are similar to* borlotti *or our pinto or cranberry beans, the beans are first cooked, then sauteed with* guanciale *and onion to make them irresistibly flavorful.*

1   CUP DRIED ROMAN, BORLOTTI, PINTO, OR CRANBERRY BEANS

1   TABLESPOON OLIVE OIL

4   OUNCES GUANCIALE (SEE INGREDIENT GUIDE ON PAGE 19), CHOPPED

1   SMALL YELLOW ONION, CHOPPED

  SALT AND FRESHLY GROUND BLACK PEPPER

Soak the beans in cold water for 8 hours or longer. Drain and discard the soaking water. Rinse under cold water and drain again. Combine the beans with 6 cups cold water in a medium saucepan over medium-high heat. When the water begins to boil, lower the heat and simmer, uncovered, about 1 hour, until the beans are tender. Drain.

Heat the olive oil in a heavy 4-quart casserole over medium heat. Add the guanciale and cook, stirring, about 5 minutes, until it is brown. It will brown quickly. Add the onion and cook about 3 minutes longer, until it begins to soften. Stir in the beans. Lower the heat and simmer together about 10 minutes. Season with salt and pepper to taste.

MAKES 4 SERVINGS

Fagioli alla veneziana

VENETIAN SWEET-AND-SOUR BEANS

The sweet-and-sour flavoring in this dish is typical of Venetian cooking. Serve these beans as a first course or as an accompaniment to grilled meat or chicken.

1   CUP DRIED FAGIOLI DI LAMON, BORLOTTI, PINTO, OR CRANBERRY BEANS

1   LARGE CLOVE GARLIC, PEELED

¼   CUP OLIVE OIL

2   ANCHOVIES PACKED IN SALT, RINSED IN COLD WATER, FILLETED, AND CHOPPED, OR 4 ANCHOVY FILLETS PACKED IN OIL, DRAINED, AND CHOPPED (SEE INGREDIENT GUIDE ON PAGE 19)

1   LARGE RED ONION, HALVED AND THINLY SLICED

¼   CUP RED WINE VINEGAR

    SALT AND FRESHLY GROUND BLACK PEPPER

8   STEMS FRESH ITALIAN FLAT-LEAF PARSLEY, LEAVES ONLY, CHOPPED

Soak the beans in cold water for 8 hours or longer. Drain and discard the soaking water. Combine the beans with the garlic and 6 cups cold water in a medium saucepan over medium-high heat. When the water begins to boil, lower the heat and simmer, uncovered, about 1 hour, until the beans are tender. Drain and discard the garlic.

Heat the oil in a large skillet over medium heat. Add the anchovies and mash with a wooden spoon. Add the onion and cook 10 minutes, until translucent. Stir in the vinegar and ½ cup cold water and cook 5 minutes. Stir in the beans, season with salt and pepper, and cook about 10 minutes longer, until the sauce is thick. Garnish with parsley.

MAKES 4 SERVINGS

CHICKPEAS BRAISED WITH SWISS CHARD

In zimino is a typical Tuscan preparation for braising with Swiss chard or spinach that I learned from Giuliano Bugialli at his cooking school outside Florence. It's also a common way to cook squid. This can be a side dish to a main course, but it's equally good as a first course.

1	CUP DRIED CHICKPEAS OR 2 CUPS COOKED CHICKPEAS, DRAINED
	SALT
2	BUNCHES GREEN OR RED SWISS CHARD, RINSED, STEMMED, AND ROUGHLY CHOPPED
¼	CUP EXTRA VIRGIN OLIVE OIL
1	LARGE CLOVE GARLIC, PEELED AND FINELY CHOPPED
1	SMALL RED ONION, CHOPPED
1	SMALL CARROT, CHOPPED
	PINCH OF PEPERONCINO (RED PEPPER FLAKES)
½	CUP DRY WHITE WINE
2	CUPS CHICKEN BROTH
1	TABLESPOON TOMATO PASTE

If you are using dried chickpeas, soak them in cold water for 8 hours or longer. Drain and discard the soaking water. Rinse under cold water and drain again. Combine the beans with 6 cups cold water in a medium saucepan over medium-high heat. When the water begins to boil, lower the heat and simmer, uncovered, about 1 hour, until the beans are tender. Season with salt, turn off the heat, and set aside.

Bring a large pot of water to a boil over high heat. Add the chard and cook 5 minutes. Drain in a colander and rinse under cold water. When cool enough to handle, take handfuls of the chard and gently squeeze out the water. Chop and set aside.

Heat the olive oil in a large saucepan over medium heat. Add the garlic, onion, carrot, and peperoncino and cook gently 2 to 3 minutes, until the vegetables begin to soften. Add the wine and let it evaporate slowly, about 10 minutes. Drain the chickpeas, add them to the pan along with the chard, and season with salt to taste. Combine the broth and tomato paste and add it to the pan. Cook, stirring, to combine the chard and chickpeas with the vegetables. Simmer about 10 minutes, until about half the broth has evaporated and the sauce is thick. Serve hot.

MAKES 4 SERVINGS

GRANDMA PISTELLI'S BEANS AND OLIVE OIL

When I visited Enzo Pistelli, a bean grower and olive oil maker in southern Umbria, his mother prepared us a lunch of the tiny white beans, fagioli del purgatorio, *that are typical of the region. This dish, which can be an accompaniment to any meal or the basis of lunch when served with some cheese and bread, couldn't be simpler. What makes the dish so memorable is the intensely flavorful Pistelli olive oil (see Ingredient Guide on page 19). If you can't find Pistelli, use any good Tuscan or Umbrian extra virgin olive oil.*

1   POUND DRIED FAGIOLI DEL PURGATORIO OR NAVY BEANS
    SALT AND FRESHLY GROUND BLACK PEPPER
½   CUP EXTRA VIRGIN OLIVE OIL, PREFERABLY PISTELLI

Soak the beans in cold water for 8 hours or longer. Drain and discard the soaking water. Rinse under cold water and drain again. Combine the beans with 8 cups cold water in a medium saucepan over medium-high heat. When the water begins to boil, lower the heat and simmer, uncovered, 30 to 45 minutes, until the beans are tender. Season with salt, remove from the heat, and allow to cool to room temperature.

When you are ready to serve, drain the beans well and transfer to a serving bowl. Season with salt, if necessary, and pepper to taste. Add the olive oil and mix well to combine.

MAKES 4 TO 6 SERVINGS

Fagioli all'uccelletto

BEANS IN TOMATO SAUCE

This is one of the most typical Tuscan preparations for beans—you find it all over the region—and it's almost always prepared with white cannellini beans. The name all'uccelletto refers to the cooking method traditionally used to prepare the uccellino, *a small game bird. This is the classic recipe; there are many variations.*

1   CUP DRIED CANNELLINI BEANS
    SALT

3   TABLESPOONS OLIVE OIL

1   LARGE CLOVE GARLIC, PEELED AND
    FINELY CHOPPED

3   LEAVES FRESH SAGE, CHOPPED

1   CUP TOMATO PUREE
    FRESHLY GROUND BLACK PEPPER

Soak the beans in cold water for 8 hours or longer. Drain and discard the soaking water. Rinse under cold water and drain again. Combine the beans with 6 cups cold water in a large saucepan over medium-high heat. When the water begins to boil, lower the heat and simmer, uncovered, about 1 hour, until the beans are tender. Season with salt, turn off the heat, and allow to cool to room temperature. Drain.

Meanwhile, heat the oil in a large saucepan over medium heat. Add garlic and sage and cook for 1 minute, being careful not to brown the garlic. Add the tomato puree and cook about 2 minutes longer. Add the beans and simmer 10 to 15 minutes. Season with salt and pepper to taste.

MAKES 4 TO 6 SERVINGS

CLASSIC OVEN-BAKED WHITE BEANS

Cooking beans in the oven instead of on the stovetop is a traditional Tuscan technique. Many Tuscans still use a fagioliera, a terra-cotta bean pot. Glazed inside but not outside, the pots are perfect for preparing beans this way. You can also use an ordinary casserole. After the beans are cooked, leave them in the pot or casserole without draining until you are ready to serve them.

2 CUPS DRIED WHITE BEANS, SUCH AS CANNELLINI, SORANINI, GREAT NORTHERN, OR NAVY

2 OUNCES PANCETTA (SEE INGREDIENT GUIDE ON PAGE 19), CUBED

3 LARGE LEAVES FRESH SAGE

1 CLOVE GARLIC, PEELED

3 TABLESPOONS EXTRA VIRGIN OLIVE OIL, PLUS MORE FOR SERVING

SALT AND FRESHLY GROUND BLACK PEPPER

Soak the beans in cold water for 8 hours or longer. Drain and discard the soaking water. Rinse under cold water and drain again.

Preheat the oven to 350 degrees.

Transfer the beans to a heavy 4-quart casserole. Add the pancetta, sage, garlic, and olive oil. Add 8 cups cold water, enough to generously cover the beans. Cover the casserole and place on the middle shelf in the oven. Cook about 1½ to 2 hours, until the beans are tender but still firm. When you are ready to serve, discard the pancetta, sage, and garlic and drain off any excess water. Season with salt and pepper. Serve the beans warm with olive oil.

MAKES 4 TO 6 SERVINGS

OVEN-BAKED WHITE BEANS FROM REGGELLO

Mario Agostinelli, a bean grower in Reggello, south of Florence, told me that this is his favorite way to prepare the little white zolfino beans he grows. His favorite cooking pot is an ovenproof glass casserole.

2   CUPS DRIED ZOLFINO, GREAT NORTHERN, OR NAVY BEANS

1   WHOLE SMALL HEAD OF GARLIC, PAPERY WHITE OUTER SKIN REMOVED, TOP ¼ INCH CUT FROM THE HEAD

3   TABLESPOONS OLIVE OIL, PLUS MORE FOR SERVING SALT AND FRESHLY GROUND BLACK PEPPER

Soak the beans in cold water for 8 hours or longer. Drain and discard the soaking water. Rinse under cold water and drain again.

Preheat the oven to 350 degrees.

Combine the beans with the garlic and olive oil in a heavy 4-quart casserole. Add about 8 cups cold water, enough to generously cover the beans. Cover the casserole and place on the middle shelf in the oven. Bake 1½ to 2 hours, until the beans are tender but still firm. Allow the beans to remain, undrained, in the casserole until you are ready to serve them. Remove and discard the garlic. Pour off any excess water. Season with salt and pepper to taste. Serve the beans warm with olive oil.

MAKES 4 SERVINGS

Lenticchie alla romana

ROMAN-STYLE LENTILS WITH PROSCIUTTO

This is a rich and tasty side dish from Rome that you can serve as an accompaniment to meat or chicken or as a main course for a light supper or lunch with a green salad. I like to serve it with roasted lamb.

1 CUP ITALIAN SMALL BROWN LENTILS OR FRENCH GREEN LENTILS

2 OUNCES PROSCIUTTO (SEE INGREDIENT GUIDE ON PAGE 19), CUT INTO SMALL DICE

1 TABLESPOON OLIVE OIL

1 MEDIUM RED ONION, FINELY CHOPPED

1 CLOVE GARLIC, PEELED AND FINELY CHOPPED

1 RIB CELERY, FINELY CHOPPED

8 STEMS FRESH ITALIAN FLAT-LEAF PARSLEY, LEAVES ONLY, CHOPPED

4 MEDIUM RIPE TOMATOES, CORED, PEELED, SEEDED, AND CHOPPED, OR ⅓ CUP TOMATO PUREE

SALT AND FRESHLY GROUND BLACK PEPPER

Put the lentils in a medium saucepan with 6 cups cold water over medium-high heat. Bring the water to a boil. Lower the heat and simmer, uncovered, about 45 minutes, until the lentils are tender. Drain in a strainer and set aside.

Meanwhile, combine the prosciutto and olive oil in a heavy 4-quart casserole and place over medium heat. Cook about 5 minutes, until the prosciutto begins to brown. Add the onion, garlic, celery, and parsley and continue cooking about 10 minutes longer, until the vegetables are lightly browned. Add the tomatoes and cook 10 minutes longer. Stir in the drained lentils, season with salt and pepper to taste, and allow to simmer gently for 10 minutes before serving.

MAKES 4 SERVINGS

Lenticchie e finocchio brasati

BRAISED LENTILS WITH FRESH FENNEL

Fresh fennel infuses this dish with a delicate but distinctive flavor that makes a perfect accompaniment to grilled fish or chicken. The recipe calls for chicken broth, but you can also use vegetable broth. I like to finely chop the vegetables all together in a food processor.

2   TABLESPOONS OLIVE OIL
1   CARROT, CHOPPED
1   ONION, CHOPPED
1   FENNEL BULB, STALKS TRIMMED AND DISCARDED, CHOPPED
1   CLOVE GARLIC, PEELED AND FINELY CHOPPED
1   CUP ITALIAN SMALL BROWN LENTILS OR FRENCH GREEN LENTILS
2   CUPS CHICKEN OR VEGETABLE BROTH
1   BAY LEAF
     SALT AND FRESHLY GROUND BLACK PEPPER

Heat the olive oil in a heavy 4-quart casserole over medium heat. Add the carrot, onion, fennel, and garlic and cook, stirring, about 5 minutes, until the vegetables begin to soften. Add the lentils, broth, bay leaf, and about 4 cups cold water and bring to a boil. Lower the heat and simmer, partially covered, about 45 minutes, until the lentils are tender but still firm. Discard the bay leaf. Season with salt and pepper to taste and serve.

MAKES 6 SERVINGS

Lenticchie alla lombardia

BRAISED LENTILS LOMBARDY-STYLE

A traditional dish that's prepared in many parts of Italy, this recipe from Lombardy is typically served as a side dish with meat or polenta.

2   TABLESPOONS OLIVE OIL

2   OUNCES PANCETTA (SEE INGREDIENT GUIDE ON PAGE 19), CUT INTO SMALL DICE

1   MEDIUM RED ONION, FINELY CHOPPED

4   LARGE LEAVES FRESH SAGE, CHOPPED

1½ CUPS ITALIAN SMALL BROWN LENTILS OR FRENCH GREEN LENTILS

    SALT

Heat the olive oil in a heavy 4-quart casserole over medium heat. Add the pancetta, onion, and sage and cook, stirring, 3 to 5 minutes, until the onion begins to soften and the pancetta begins to render its fat. Add the lentils and 4 cups cold water and raise the heat to medium-high. When the water begins to boil, lower the heat and simmer, uncovered, about 45 minutes, until the lentils are tender. Add salt to taste.

MAKES 6 SERVINGS

Fasoi in potacin

SLOWLY SIMMERED BEANS IN TOMATO SAUCE

In the Veneto, this dish is called fasoi *("beans" in the local dialect). The beans are simmered slowly with onions and tomato puree for several hours, resulting in a marvelously flavored appetizer or accompaniment to grilled meat.*

1   CUP DRIED BORLOTTI, PINTO, OR CRANBERRY
      BEANS
2   TABLESPOONS OLIVE OIL
1   MEDIUM RED ONION, HALVED AND THINLY SLICED
1   CUP TOMATO PUREE
      SALT

Soak the beans in cold water for 8 hours or longer. Drain and discard the soaking water. Rinse under cold water and drain again.

Heat the olive oil in a heavy 4-quart casserole over medium heat. Add the onion and cook about 3 minutes, until it begins to soften. Add the beans, tomato puree, and 6 cups cold water. Raise the heat to medium-high and bring the liquid to a boil. Lower the heat and simmer, partially covered, 2 to 3 hours, until the beans are tender and the tomato sauce is thick. Add salt to taste.

MAKES 4 SERVINGS

Zuppe di Fagioli
BEAN SOUPS

There is no part of Italian cooking more diverse than the exuberant variety of bean soups. Italian cooks generally classify soups three ways. In *minestre* the various ingredients are distinct from the broth in which they cook; *zuppe* are thick soups often made with beans and grains; and *passati*— also called *creme* or *vellutate*—are pureed, creamy, smooth soups. These terms are loosely applied. Some main-course dishes may be called *zuppe* or *minestre* but are actually stews. What we think of as *minestrone* is, at its simplest, a vegetable and bean *minestra*. There are dozens if not hundreds of versions, as *minestrone* tends to differ from region to region and even town to town.

Many of these soups call for pancetta or prosciutto. While the meat is essential to the authentic taste of the soup, you can make any of these recipes vegetarian. Simply omit the meat, substitute 2 tablespoons olive oil, and use vegetable broth instead of water.

This chapter offers soups to suit every palate and any occasion. Still, it's a small sampling from the abundant assortment of bean soups that can be found in the bean cuisine of Italy.

Minestrone genovese

GENOA-STYLE MINESTRONE WITH PESTO

This soup captures all the flavors of the Italian Riviera, with lots of greens and pesto. Pesto varies throughout Liguria. The pesto called for here is prepared without pignoli or nuts of any kind. You get a lot of cheese flavor from the parmigiano rind cooked in the soup.

MINESTRONE

1 CUP DRIED BORLOTTI, PINTO, OR CRANBERRY BEANS

¼ CUP OLIVE OIL

1 MEDIUM RED ONION, CHOPPED

1 MEDIUM LEEK, ROOT END REMOVED, RINSED UNDER COLD WATER AND CHOPPED

1 MEDIUM CARROT, CHOPPED

1 RIB CELERY, CHOPPED

1 LARGE CLOVE GARLIC, PEELED AND FINELY CHOPPED

2 SMALL ZUCCHINI, CUT INTO SMALL DICE

½ SMALL HEAD SAVOY CABBAGE, SHREDDED

¼ POUND GREEN BEANS, ENDS TRIMMED, CUT INTO 1-INCH PIECES

3 LARGE GREEN SWISS CHARD LEAVES, RINSED, STEMMED, AND COARSELY CHOPPED

1 MEDIUM YUKON GOLD OR YELLOW FINN POTATO, PEELED AND DICED

1 PIECE (APPROXIMATELY 3 INCHES BY 2 INCHES) PARMIGIANO CHEESE RIND (SEE INGREDIENT GUIDE ON PAGE 19)

SALT AND FRESHLY GROUND BLACK PEPPER

1 CUP DRIED TUBETTI OR OTHER SMALL MACARONI

PESTO SAUCE

1	CUP PACKED FRESH BASIL LEAVES
1	CUP PACKED FRESH ITALIAN FLAT-LEAF PARSLEY, LEAVES ONLY, CHOPPED
1	CLOVE GARLIC, PEELED
½	CUP OLIVE OIL
	GRATED PARMIGIANO CHEESE, FOR SERVING

To prepare the minestrone: Soak the beans in cold water for 8 hours or longer. Drain and discard the soaking water. Rinse under cold water and drain again.

Heat the olive oil in a heavy 6-quart soup pot or casserole over medium heat. Add the onion, leek, carrot, celery, and garlic and cook, stirring, about 3 minutes, until the vegetables begin to soften. Add the soaked beans, zucchini, cabbage, green beans, chard, and potato. Mix well to combine. Stir in 8 cups cold water. Raise the heat to high and bring the water to a boil. Lower the heat and simmer, partially covered, about 45 minutes, stirring occasionally. Add the cheese rind and continue cooking 15 minutes longer. The rind will begin to melt and dissolve into the soup. At this point, the soup should be thick and the beans tender. Season with salt and pepper to taste.

To prepare the pesto: Combine the basil, parsley, and garlic in a food processor or blender. Turn the machine on and off a few times to chop the ingredients. With the machine running, add the olive oil in a steady stream and continue processing until the mixture resembles a smooth paste. Set aside.

Fifteen minutes before serving, reheat the soup over medium-high heat. When it comes to a low boil, add the pasta. Continue cooking, stirring frequently to prevent the pasta from sticking to the bottom of the pot, 10 to 12 minutes, until the pasta is tender but firm to the bite, al dente. Stir in the pesto and serve with parmigiano cheese.

MAKES 6 SERVINGS

ABRUZZI-STYLE MINESTRONE WITH CANNELLINI, CHICKPEAS, AND LENTILS

Also called virtu *in the regional dialect, this hearty vegetable soup from the region of Abruzzo, southeast of Rome, is prepared in the early spring, when fresh fava beans and peas are in season. It's traditionally made with meat broth, including the meat from the bones used to make the broth. You can also use chicken or vegetable broth.*

½ CUP DRIED CANNELLINI OR GREAT NORTHERN BEANS

½ CUP CHICKPEAS

½ CUP ITALIAN SMALL BROWN LENTILS OR FRENCH GREEN LENTILS

6 CUPS MEAT, CHICKEN, OR VEGETABLE BROTH

2 MEDIUM RED ONIONS, CHOPPED

1 LARGE CARROT, CHOPPED

1 RIB CELERY, CHOPPED

3 STEMS FRESH MARJORAM

¼ CUP OLIVE OIL

8 STEMS FRESH ITALIAN FLAT-LEAF PARSLEY, LEAVES ONLY, CHOPPED

3 FRESH PLUM TOMATOES, CORED, SEEDED, AND CHOPPED

1 LARGE CLOVE GARLIC, PEELED

1 CUP PEELED FRESH FAVA BEANS (ABOUT 2 POUNDS IN THEIR PODS)

1 CUP FRESH PEAS

2 LARGE GREEN SWISS CHARD LEAVES, RINSED, STEMMED, AND CHOPPED

1 CUP DRIED SMALL TUBULAR PASTA SUCH AS TUBETTINI OR DITALINI

SALT AND FRESHLY GROUND BLACK PEPPER

½ CUP GRATED PARMIGIANO CHEESE

Soak the beans and lentils together in cold water for 8 hours or longer. Drain and discard the soaking water. Rinse under cold water and drain again. Combine the beans with 6 cups cold water in a heavy 6-quart soup pot or casserole over medium-high heat. When the water begins to boil, lower the heat and simmer, uncovered, about 45 minutes. The beans will still be quite firm. Drain the beans in a colander and return them to the pot.

Add the broth, 1 onion, the carrot, celery, and marjoram and place over medium-high heat. When the broth begins to simmer, lower the heat and continue cooking about 30 minutes longer, or until the beans are tender.

Meanwhile, heat the olive oil in a medium skillet over medium heat. Add the remaining onion, the parsley, tomatoes, and garlic and cook, stirring, about 5 minutes, until the vegetables have softened. Add them to the soup with the fava beans, peas, chard, and pasta and continue cooking, stirring frequently to prevent the pasta from sticking to the bottom of the pot, 10 to 12 minutes longer, until the pasta is tender but firm to the bite, al dente. Season with salt and pepper to taste. Serve with parmigiano cheese.

MAKES 6 SERVINGS

TUSCAN-STYLE MINESTRONE WITH VEGETABLES AND CANNELLINI

This traditional minestrone from Tuscany is fresh and flavorful, but I think it's always a little better the day after you prepare it. In the summer, this soup is delicious when served at room temperature with a drizzle of olive oil on top. It's light and perfect warm-weather fare.

1 CUP DRIED CANNELLINI OR GREAT NORTHERN BEANS
  SALT
½ CUP OLIVE OIL, PLUS MORE FOR SERVING
1 MEDIUM RED ONION, CHOPPED
½ POUND GREEN CABBAGE, SHREDDED

1 BUNCH GREEN SWISS CHARD, RINSED, STEMMED, AND ROUGHLY CHOPPED
1 RIB CELERY, CUT INTO ½-INCH PIECES
3 CARROTS, CUT INTO SMALL PIECES
3 ZUCCHINI, CUT INTO 1-INCH PIECES
¼ POUND GREEN BEANS, ENDS TRIMMED, CUT INTO 2 OR 3 PIECES
2 POTATOES, PEELED AND DICED
8 LARGE LEAVES FRESH BASIL, CHOPPED
1 TABLESPOON TOMATO PASTE
2 CUPS CHICKEN OR VEGETABLE BROTH
  FRESHLY GROUND BLACK PEPPER

Soak the beans in cold water for 8 hours or longer. Drain and discard the soaking water. Rinse under cold water and drain again. Combine the beans with 6 cups cold water in a medium saucepan over medium heat. When the water begins to boil, lower the heat and simmer, uncovered, about 1 hour, until the beans are tender. Season with salt, turn off the heat, and set aside.

Heat the olive oil in a heavy 6-quart soup pot or casserole over medium heat. Add the onion and cook, stirring, about 3 minutes, until it begins to soften. Add the cabbage, chard, celery, carrots, zucchini, green beans, potatoes, and basil. Stir the tomato paste into the broth and add to the pot. Strain the cooked beans and add them with 2 cups of the cooking liquid to the pot with the vegetables. Season with salt and pepper to taste. Raise the heat to medium-high and bring the liquid to a boil. Lower the heat and simmer, partially covered, 30 minutes.

Turn off the heat and allow the soup to stand for at least 5 minutes before serving. Add a drizzle of olive oil to each serving.

MAKES 6 SERVINGS

MINESTRONE WITH CANNELLINI AND TUSCAN BREAD

Bread is one of the cornerstones of the cuisine of Tuscany. This wonderful vegetable soup from the Tuscan hills is served over a thick slice of toast. Use day-old country-style bread.

2 CUPS DRIED CANNELLINI OR GREAT NORTHERN BEANS

SALT

¼ CUP OLIVE OIL, PLUS MORE FOR SERVING

4 OUNCES PANCETTA (SEE INGREDIENT GUIDE ON PAGE 19), CHOPPED

1 MEDIUM RED ONION, CHOPPED

1 RIB CELERY, CHOPPED

10 STEMS FRESH ITALIAN FLAT-LEAF PARSLEY, LEAVES ONLY, CHOPPED

10 LEAVES FRESH BASIL, CHOPPED

4 CLOVES GARLIC, PEELED, 3 FINELY CHOPPED, 1 WHOLE

PINCH OF PEPERONCINO (RED PEPPER FLAKES)

½ POUND GREEN CABBAGE LEAVES

1 BUNCH KALE, STEMMED

1 POUND CANNED WHOLE PEELED TOMATOES, DRAINED, SEEDED, AND COARSELY CHOPPED

FRESHLY GROUND BLACK PEPPER

6 SLICES TUSCAN OR OTHER RUSTIC COUNTRY BREAD

Soak the beans in cold water for 8 hours or longer. Drain and discard the soaking water. Rinse under cold water and drain again. Combine the beans with 8 cups cold water in a heavy 6-quart soup pot or casserole over medium-high heat. When the water begins to boil, lower the heat and simmer, uncovered, about 1 hour, until the beans are tender. Season with salt, turn off the heat, and set aside.

Heat the olive oil in a large saucepan. Add the pancetta and cook, stirring, about 10 minutes, until it begins to brown. Add the onion, celery, parsley, basil, chopped garlic, and peperoncino. Saute slowly over medium-low heat.

Meanwhile, bring a large pot of water to a boil over high heat. Cook the cabbage and kale in boiling water for 15 minutes. Drain and rinse under cold water. When they are cool enough to handle, gently squeeze the water from the kale and cabbage with your hands, then chop and add to the onion and pancetta mixture. Stir in the tomatoes and continue cooking, slowly, for 10 minutes longer. Transfer to the pot with the beans and turn the heat to medium-high. When the soup begins to boil, lower the heat and simmer an additional 40 minutes to combine the flavors. Season with salt and pepper to taste.

Toast the bread until it is lightly browned. Rub the toast with the remaining whole garlic clove and place each slice in individual soup bowls. Drizzle some olive oil over the toast, ladle the soup over the bread, and serve.

MAKES 6 SERVINGS

LIVORNO-STYLE MINESTRONE WITH CANNELLINI AND BREAD

This is a recipe from the coast of Tuscany near the port city of Livorno. It is a wonderful soup to prepare in the late summer, when the vegetables can be bought fresh at a local farm stand or farmers' market. The addition of bread to the soup makes this a satisfying and filling dish.

1 POUND DRIED CANNELLINI OR GREAT NORTHERN BEANS

3 CLOVES GARLIC, PEELED, 1 WHOLE, 2 FINELY CHOPPED

5 TABLESPOONS OLIVE OIL

4 CARROTS, CHOPPED

3 RIBS CELERY, CHOPPED

1 LARGE RED ONION, CHOPPED

½ POUND SAVOY CABBAGE, SHREDDED

½ POUND ZUCCHINI, CHOPPED

¼ POUND GREEN BEANS, ENDS TRIMMED, CUT INTO 1-INCH PIECES

1 MEDIUM YUKON GOLD OR YELLOW FINN POTATO, PEELED AND CHOPPED

1 POUND CANNED WHOLE PEELED TOMATOES, SEEDED AND CHOPPED, WITH THEIR JUICE

8 GREEN SWISS CHARD LEAVES (2 BUNCHES), RINSED, STEMMED, AND ROUGHLY CHOPPED

8 LEAVES FRESH BASIL

8 STEMS FRESH ITALIAN FLAT-LEAF PARSLEY, LEAVES ONLY, CHOPPED

SALT AND FRESHLY GROUND BLACK PEPPER

1 POUND STALE TUSCAN OR OTHER RUSTIC COUNTRY BREAD, CUT INTO 1-INCH CUBES

GRATED PARMIGIANO CHEESE, FOR SERVING

Soak the beans in cold water for 8 hours or longer. Drain and discard the soaking water. Rinse under cold water and drain again. Combine the beans with the whole clove of garlic, 1 tablespoon olive oil, and 8 cups cold water in a heavy large saucepan over medium-high heat. When the water begins to boil, lower the heat and simmer, uncovered, about 1 hour, until the beans are tender. Drain the beans and reserve the bean water. Transfer half the beans to a food processor or blender and process until smooth. Set aside.

Meanwhile, heat the remaining 4 tablespoons olive oil in a heavy 6-quart soup pot or casserole over medium heat. Add the carrots, celery, onion, and the chopped garlic and cook about 3 minutes, until the vegetables begin to soften. Add the cabbage, zucchini, green beans, potato, tomatoes with their juice, and all the beans and stir well to combine. Stir in the chard and add 6 cups of the bean-cooking water. If there isn't enough bean water, add plain water or broth. Place the pot over medium-high heat and bring to a boil. Lower the heat and simmer, partially covered, about 45 minutes. Stir in the basil and parsley and season with salt and pepper to taste. Add the bread, stir to combine, and turn off the heat. Let the soup stand, covered, for 15 minutes. Serve with parmigiano cheese.

MAKES 6 SERVINGS

MINESTRONE OF CICERCHIE

This recipe comes from a restaurant in Assisi, one of Umbria's most beautiful hill towns. Cicerchie are a type of chickpea traditionally grown in the south of Italy, but Umbrian growers produce them, too. In Umbria, cicerchie are small, about the size of a corn kernel. The southern variety is much larger.

2	CUPS CICERCHIE OR CHICKPEAS
1	RIB CELERY, FINELY CHOPPED
1	MEDIUM CARROT, FINELY CHOPPED
½	CUP OLIVE OIL
1	MEDIUM RED ONION, FINELY CHOPPED
3	YUKON GOLD OR YELLOW FINN POTATOES, PEELED AND CUT INTO SMALL DICE
	SALT AND FRESHLY GROUND BLACK PEPPER
1	POUND (ABOUT 6) FRESH PLUM TOMATOES, CORED, SEEDED, AND CHOPPED
15	STEMS FRESH ITALIAN FLAT-LEAF PARSLEY, LEAVES ONLY, FINELY CHOPPED
	EXTRA VIRGIN OLIVE OIL, FOR SERVING
	GRATED PARMIGIANO CHEESE, FOR SERVING

Soak the cicerchie in cold water for 8 hours or longer. Drain and discard the soaking water. Rinse under cold water and drain again. Combine the beans with the celery, carrot, and 10 cups cold water in a heavy 6-quart soup pot or casserole over medium-high heat. When the water begines to boil, lower the heat and simmer, stirring occasionally, 1 to 2 hours, until the beans are tender.

Heat the olive oil in a medium saucepan over medium heat. Add the onion and potatoes and cook, stirring, about 5 minutes; add to the beans. Continue cooking about 30 minutes longer. The beans should be quite tender. Season with salt and pepper to taste. Stir in the tomatoes and parsley and cook 5 minutes longer. Serve with a drizzle of extra virgin olive oil and parmigiano cheese.

MAKES 6 SERVINGS

SOUP OF LENTILS AND SWISS CHARD

A simple but intensely good soup that you can prepare quickly.
Lentils require no soaking.

1	CUP ITALIAN SMALL BROWN LENTILS OR FRENCH GREEN LENTILS
	SALT
1	CUP TOMATO PUREE
2	BUNCHES GREEN SWISS CHARD, RINSED, STEMMED, AND COARSELY CHOPPED
3	TABLESPOONS OLIVE OIL, PLUS MORE FOR SERVING
4	SLICES (½ INCH EACH) STALE OR LIGHTLY TOASTED RUSTIC COUNTRY BREAD

Rinse the lentils under cold water and drain. Combine the lentils with 4 cups cold water in a heavy 6-quart soup pot or casserole and place over medium-high heat. When the water begins to boil, lower the heat and simmer, uncovered, about 45 minutes, until the lentils are tender. Season with salt to taste and add the tomato puree, chard, and 3 tablespoons olive oil. Cover the pot and continue cooking, stirring occasionally, for 40 minutes.

To serve, place a slice of the bread in each bowl and ladle the soup over the bread.

MAKES 6 SERVINGS

Minestra di scarola e fagioli cannellini

SOUP OF ESCAROLE AND CANNELLINI

This recipe is Sardinian, but similar soups are prepared elsewhere in Italy. It's traditionally served over bread; I like to make the soup somewhat smooth and serve the bread on the side.

1   CUP DRIED CANNELLINI OR GREAT NORTHERN BEANS
1   MEDIUM RED ONION, FINELY CHOPPED
     SALT
¼   CUP OLIVE OIL, PLUS MORE FOR SERVING
2   CLOVES GARLIC, PEELED AND FINELY CHOPPED
     PINCH OF PEPERONCINO (RED PEPPER FLAKES)
2   BUNCHES FRESH ESCAROLE, ROOT END TRIMMED, LEAVES RINSED IN COLD WATER, AND COARSELY CHOPPED

Soak the beans in cold water for 8 hours. Drain and discard the soaking water. Rinse under cold water and drain again. Combine the beans with the onion in a medium saucepan with 6 cups cold water over medium-high heat. When the water begins to boil, lower the heat and simmer, uncovered, about 1 hour, until tender. Season with salt, and drain and reserve the cooking liquid.

Heat the olive oil in a heavy 6-quart soup pot or casserole over medium heat. Add the garlic, peperoncino, and escarole and saute 7 to 10 minutes, until the escarole is wilted. Add the beans and 3 cups of the cooking liquid and season with salt to taste. When the soup begins to boil, lower the heat and simmer 20 minutes longer. Transfer 3 cups of soup to a food processor or blender, and process until smooth. Return the pureed soup to the pot and heat through before serving.

MAKES 6 SERVINGS

LIVORNO-STYLE CHICKPEA SOUP

A cacciucco *is a traditional fish soup originally from the Mediterranean port city of Livorno that's now widely prepared all along the Tuscan coast. It's typically more of a stew than a soup, and it should be thick and rich. This version with chickpeas and chard gets a lot of its flavor from anchovies.*

2 CUPS CHICKPEAS

3 TABLESPOONS OLIVE OIL, PLUS MORE FOR SERVING

3 ANCHOVIES PACKED IN SALT, RINSED IN COLD WATER, FILLETED, AND CHOPPED, OR 6 ANCHOVY FILLETS PACKED IN OIL, DRAINED AND CHOPPED (SEE INGREDIENT GUIDE ON PAGE 19)

1 MEDIUM RED ONION, FINELY CHOPPED

1 LARGE CLOVE GARLIC, PEELED AND FINELY CHOPPED

3 LARGE GREEN SWISS CHARD LEAVES, RINSED, STEMMED, AND CHOPPED

2 TABLESPOONS TOMATO PASTE

SALT AND FRESHLY GROUND BLACK PEPPER

GRATED AGED PECORINO TOSCANO CHEESE, FOR SERVING

Soak the chickpeas in cold water for 8 hours or longer. Drain and discard the soaking water. Rinse under cold water and drain again.

Heat the olive oil in a large 6-quart soup pot or casserole over medium heat. Add the anchovies and mash them into the oil with a wooden spoon. Stir in the onion and garlic and cook, stirring, about 3 minutes, until the onion begins to soften. Add the chard and beans. Dissolve the tomato paste in 1 cup water and add it with 7 cups cold water to the beans. Raise the heat to medium-high and bring the water to a boil. Lower the heat and simmer, stirring occasionally, 1 to 1½ hours, until the chickpeas are tender.

Transfer 2 cups of soup to a food processor or blender. Process until smooth. Return the pureed soup to the pot, season with salt and pepper to taste, and cook about 10 minutes longer.

Ladle into bowls and add a drizzle of olive oil and pecorino toscano cheese to each serving.

MAKES 6 SERVINGS

SOUP OF RICE AND WHITE BEANS

Rice and beans are not generally associated with Italian cooking. But Italy grows many varieties of rice, and soups with rice and beans are prepared in the northern regions.

This rustic soup from Tuscany can be prepared ahead of time, but add the rice and finish cooking just when you are ready to serve it.

2   CUPS DRIED CANNELLINI, SORANINI, GREAT NORTHERN, OR NAVY BEANS

2   CLOVES GARLIC, PEELED

3   TABLESPOONS OLIVE OIL

4   OUNCES PROSCIUTTO (SEE INGREDIENT GUIDE ON PAGE 19), FINELY CHOPPED (YOU CAN USE A FOOD PROCESSOR)

1   MEDIUM RED ONION, FINELY CHOPPED

1   RIB CELERY, FINELY CHOPPED

15 STEMS FRESH ITALIAN FLAT-LEAF PARSLEY, LEAVES ONLY, CHOPPED

3   LEAVES FRESH BASIL, FINELY CHOPPED

PINCH OF PEPERONCINO (RED PEPPER FLAKES)

2   CUPS CANNED CHOPPED TOMATOES, WITH THEIR JUICE

SALT

½   CUP ARBORIO OR OTHER ITALIAN RICE (SEE INGREDIENT GUIDE ON PAGE 19)

Soak the beans in cold water for 8 hours or longer. Drain and discard the soaking water. Rinse under cold water and drain again. Combine the beans with 1 clove of the garlic and 8 cups water in a heavy 6-quart soup pot or casserole over medium-high heat. When the water begins to boil, lower the heat and simmer, uncovered, about 1 hour, until the beans are tender.

Meanwhile, heat the olive oil in a large skillet over medium heat. Add the prosciutto, onion, celery, parsley, basil, and peperoncino and cook, stirring frequently, about 10 minutes, until the onion and celery are soft and the prosciutto is beginning to turn brown. Add the tomatoes and continue cooking, stirring occasionally, 15 to 20 minutes longer, until the mixture is the consistency of a thick sauce. When the beans are ready, add the tomato sauce to the beans, season with salt to taste, and continue cooking 10 minutes longer. Stir in the rice and continue cooking 20 minutes longer, until the rice is tender but firm to the bite, al dente. Serve immediately.

MAKES 6 SERVINGS

Zuppa toscana di fagioli

TUSCAN BEAN SOUP

This is a thick, marvelous soup that's typical of the cuisine of Tuscany, with a lot of flavor from a variety of different beans. You can change the quantities of the individual beans if you don't have one on hand or prefer one bean to another.

⅓ CUP DRIED CANNELLINI OR GREAT NORTHERN BEANS

⅓ CUP DRIED BORLOTTI, PINTO, OR CRANBERRY BEANS

⅓ CUP CHICKPEAS

¼ CUP DRIED BLACK-EYED PEAS

½ CUP DRIED GREEN SPLIT PEAS

½ CUP ITALIAN SMALL BROWN LENTILS OR FRENCH GREEN LENTILS

2 TABLESPOONS OLIVE OIL, PLUS MORE FOR SERVING

4 OUNCES PROSCIUTTO (SEE INGREDIENT GUIDE ON PAGE 19), FINELY CHOPPED (YOU CAN USE A FOOD PROCESSOR)

1 MEDIUM RED ONION, CHOPPED

1 CARROT, CHOPPED

1 RIB CELERY, CHOPPED

6 LEAVES FRESH SAGE, CHOPPED

1 LARGE CLOVE GARLIC, PEELED AND FINELY CHOPPED

SALT AND FRESHLY GROUND BLACK PEPPER

Soak the beans together in cold water for 8 hours or longer. Drain and discard the soaking water. Rinse under cold water and drain again.

Heat the olive oil in a heavy 6-quart soup pot or casserole over medium heat. Add the prosciutto and cook, stirring, about 5 minutes, until the meat begins to brown. Add the onion, carrot, celery, sage, and garlic and saute about 3 minutes, until the vegetables begin to soften. Add the beans and 8 cups cold water. Raise the heat to high and bring the water to a boil. Lower the heat and simmer, partially covered, about 1½ hours, until the beans are tender and the soup is thick. Season with salt and pepper to taste and cook about 10 minutes longer.

Ladle the soup into bowls and add a drizzle of olive oil to each serving.

MAKES 6 SERVINGS

Zuppa di fagioli alla fiorentina

FLORENTINE CANNELLINI AND KALE SOUP

A classic Tuscan recipe from Florence, this soup is traditionally prepared with the bone from a prosciutto ham and cavolo nero, an Italian cabbage with dark green leaves and a slightly bitter taste that resembles kale. The closest American counterpart is dinosaur, also called Tuscan, kale, but you can use any green kale. Serve this soup over lightly toasted country-style bread and generously sprinkle some parmigiano on top.

1	CUP DRIED CANNELLINI OR GREAT NORTHERN BEANS
6	TABLESPOONS OLIVE OIL
1	SMALL RED ONION, FINELY CHOPPED
4	CLOVES GARLIC, PEELED AND FINELY CHOPPED

1	RIB CELERY, FINELY CHOPPED
1	MEDIUM CARROT, FINELY CHOPPED
1	SMALL RIPE TOMATO, CORED, SEEDED, AND CHOPPED
1	SMALL LEEK, WHITE PART ONLY, RINSED BETWEEN THE LAYERS AND CHOPPED
2	OUNCES PROSCIUTTO (SEE INGREDIENT GUIDE ON PAGE 19), CUT INTO SMALL PIECES
1	BUNCH GREEN KALE, STEMMED AND COARSELY CHOPPED
1	STEM FRESH ROSEMARY, LEAVES ONLY, CHOPPED
4	STEMS FRESH THYME, CHOPPED
4	SLICES (1 INCH EACH) TUSCAN OR OTHER RUSTIC COUNTRY BREAD
	GRATED PARMIGIANO CHEESE, FOR SERVING

Soak the beans in cold water for 8 hours or longer. Drain and discard the soaking water. Rinse under cold water and drain again.

Heat 2 tablespoons olive oil in a heavy 6-quart soup pot or casserole over medium heat. Add the onion, 1 chopped clove of garlic, the celery, carrot, tomato, and leek and cook about 3 minutes, until the vegetables begin to soften. Add the beans, prosciutto, and 8 cups cold water. When the water begins to boil, lower the heat and simmer, uncovered, about 1 hour, until the beans are tender. Transfer 2 cups of the soup to a blender or food processor and process until smooth. Return the pureed soup to the pot, add the kale, and continue cooking about 20 minutes longer.

Meanwhile, heat the remaining 4 tablespoons olive oil in a small saucepan over medium-low heat. Add the remaining chopped garlic, rosemary, and thyme and cook slowly and gently, about 10 minutes, being careful not to burn the garlic.

When the soup is done, add the garlic and herb mixture and cook an additional 5 minutes.

Toast the bread until it is lightly browned. Place a slice in each soup bowl. Spoon the soup over the bread and top with parmigiano cheese.

MAKES 6 SERVINGS

SOUP OF CANNELLINI AND GREENS

This Ligurian soup is traditionally prepared with borragine, *what Italians call* preboggin, *a leafy green that grows plentifully in Italy and in England but isn't available in the United States. Red or green Swiss chard is a good substitute. This simple soup calls for lots of olive oil to give it a rich taste.*

1   CUP DRIED CANNELLINI OR GREAT NORTHERN BEANS

3   CLOVES GARLIC, PEELED, 1 WHOLE, 2 FINELY CHOPPED

2   STEMS FRESH ROSEMARY, 1 WHOLE, 1 LEAVES ONLY, CHOPPED

½   CUP (APPROXIMATELY) OLIVE OIL

2   BUNCHES RED OR GREEN SWISS CHARD, RINSED, STEMMED, AND CHOPPED

    SALT AND FRESHLY GROUND BLACK PEPPER

3   LARGE LEAVES FRESH BASIL, CHOPPED

Soak the beans in cold water for 8 hours or longer. Drain and discard the soaking water. Rinse under cold water and drain again.

Combine the beans with the whole clove of garlic, the whole stem of rosemary, and 1 tablespoon olive oil in a heavy 6-quart soup pot or casserole with 8 cups cold water over medium-high heat. When the water begins to boil, lower the heat and simmer, partially covered, about 1 hour, until the beans are tender. Discard the rosemary stem. Add the chard and continue cooking, stirring occasionally, 20 minutes longer. Transfer about 2 cups of the soup to a food processor or blender. Process until smooth and add it back to the pot.

Heat ⅓ cup olive oil in a small saucepan over medium-low heat. Add the chopped garlic, chopped rosemary, and basil. Simmer 1 to 2 minutes, being careful not to burn the garlic, then add to the pot of soup. Continue cooking about 5 minutes longer. Season to taste with salt and pepper and serve.

MAKES 6 SERVINGS

Zuppa di ceci con funghi porcini secchi

CHICKPEA SOUP WITH DRIED PORCINI MUSHROOMS

Mushrooms and beans are a common combination in many parts of Italy. When you sample this earthy, rich, and flavorful soup, you'll understand why.

1½ CUPS CHICKPEAS

1 CUP DRIED CANNELLINI OR GREAT NORTHERN BEANS

2 BAY LEAVES

6 TABLESPOONS OLIVE OIL, PLUS MORE FOR SERVING

2 CLOVES GARLIC, PEELED, 1 WHOLE, 1 CHOPPED

SALT

1 OUNCE DRIED PORCINI MUSHROOMS (SEE INGREDIENT GUIDE ON PAGE 19)

1 MEDIUM RED ONION, CHOPPED

1 SMALL CARROT, CHOPPED

1 RIB CELERY, CHOPPED

1 GREEN SWISS CHARD LEAF, RINSED, STEMMED, AND CHOPPED

½ CUP TOMATO PUREE

FRESHLY GROUND BLACK PEPPER

Soak the chickpeas and cannellini beans together in cold water for 8 hours or longer. Drain and discard the soaking water. Rinse under cold water and drain again. Combine the chickpeas and beans with the bay leaves, 2 tablespoons olive oil, the whole clove of garlic, and 8 cups cold water in a heavy 6-quart soup pot or casserole over medium-high heat. When the water begins to boil, lower the heat and simmer, uncovered, about 1 hour, or until the chickpeas are tender. Season with salt, turn off the heat, and set aside.

Meanwhile, soak the mushrooms in 2 cups warm water for 30 minutes. Drain and reserve 1 cup of the soaking liquid, strain it through several pieces of paper towel, and set aside. Finely chop the mushrooms.

Heat the remaining 4 tablespoons olive oil in a heavy medium skillet over medium heat. Add the onion, carrot, celery, chard, chopped garlic, and mushrooms and cook, stirring frequently, about 3 minutes, until the onion begins to soften. Stir in the tomato puree and the reserved mushroom liquid and continue cooking about 10 minutes longer, until slightly thickened. Transfer to the pot with the beans. Place over medium heat and continue cooking about 30 minutes longer. Season with salt and pepper to taste. Transfer 2 cups of the soup to a food processor or blender and process until smooth. Add it back to the pot and continue cooking 10 to 15 minutes longer, until the soup is thick.

Serve with a drizzle of olive oil on each serving.

MAKES 6 SERVINGS

SOUP OF CICERCHIE AND FENNEL

This coarse, hearty soup from Umbria is traditionally prepared with locally grown cicerchie, a variety of chickpeas that look like dried corn kernels. They are more commonly found in Southern Italy, where the varieties grown are usually larger than those from Umbria. If you can't find cicerchie, use chickpeas.

2	CUPS CICERCHIE OR CHICKPEAS
4	OUNCES PANCETTA (SEE INGREDIENT GUIDE ON PAGE 19), CHOPPED
2	TABLESPOONS OLIVE OIL
1	MEDIUM RED ONION, FINELY CHOPPED
2	CLOVES GARLIC, PEELED AND FINELY CHOPPED
1	BULB FENNEL, STALKS AND LEAVES REMOVED, FINELY CHOPPED
5	STEMS FRESH ITALIAN FLAT-LEAF PARSLEY, LEAVES ONLY, CHOPPED
1	CUP CANNED CHOPPED TOMATOES
	SALT AND FRESHLY GROUND BLACK PEPPER
6	SLICES (½ INCH THICK) STALE RUSTIC COUNTRY BREAD

Soak the beans in cold water for 8 hours or longer. Drain and discard the soaking water. Rinse under cold water and drain again.

Combine the pancetta and olive oil in a heavy 6-quart soup pot or casserole over medium heat. Cook, stirring occasionally, about 10 minutes, until the pancetta is beginning to brown. Add the onion, garlic, fennel, and parsley and continue cooking, stirring, about 3 minutes, until the vegetables begin to soften. Stir in the tomatoes, the beans, and 8 cups cold water. Raise the heat to high. When the water begins to boil, lower the heat and simmer, uncovered, about 1 hour, until the beans are tender.

Transfer 3 cups of the soup to a food processor or blender and process until smooth. Return the soup to the pot, season with salt and pepper to taste, and continue cooking about 10 minutes longer.

To serve, place a slice of bread in each soup bowl and ladle the soup over the top.

MAKES 6 SERVINGS

Zuppa di lenticchie

LENTIL SOUP

This recipe from Tuscany is quick and simple to prepare. The chopped parsley and garlic added at the end of cooking add a rush of flavor.

2	CUPS ITALIAN SMALL BROWN LENTILS OR FRENCH GREEN LENTILS
2	CLOVES GARLIC, PEELED, 1 WHOLE, 1 CHOPPED
½	CUP CANNED CHOPPED TOMATOES, WITH THEIR JUICE
	SALT AND FRESHLY GROUND BLACK PEPPER
8	STEMS FRESH ITALIAN FLAT-LEAF PARSLEY, LEAVES ONLY, CHOPPED
¼	CUP EXTRA VIRGIN OLIVE OIL

Rinse the lentils under cold water and drain. Place them in a heavy 6-quart soup pot or casserole. Add the whole clove of garlic, the tomatoes with their juice, and 6 cups cold water. Place over high heat and bring the water to a boil. Lower the heat and simmer, partially covered, for 45 minutes to 1 hour, until the lentils are tender and the soup is slightly thickened.

Transfer 2 cups of the soup to a food processor or blender, or use an immersion hand blender, and process until smooth. Return the pureed soup to the pot, season with salt and pepper to taste, and add the chopped garlic, parsley, and olive oil. Simmer about 10 minutes longer to incorporate the flavors, and serve.

MAKES 6 SERVINGS

Zuppa di lenticchie e funghi

SOUP OF LENTILS AND MUSHROOMS

This recipe from southern Italy has an earthy aroma and a wonderful, rich taste that captures the essence of wild mushrooms just collected from the forest.

1 OUNCE DRIED PORCINI MUSHROOMS (SEE INGREDIENT GUIDE ON PAGE 19)
1 CUP ITALIAN SMALL BROWN LENTILS OR FRENCH GREEN LENTILS
1 RIB CELERY, FINELY CHOPPED
1 SMALL RED ONION, FINELY CHOPPED
1 PLUM TOMATO, CORED, SEEDED, AND CHOPPED
2 BAY LEAVES
   SALT
¼ CUP OLIVE OIL
1 CLOVE GARLIC, PEELED
   PINCH OF PEPERONCINO (RED PEPPER FLAKES)
½ POUND FRESH OYSTER MUSHROOMS, QUARTERED

Soak the porcini in 2 cups warm water for 30 minutes. Drain and chop. Combine the porcini with the lentils, celery, onion, tomato, and bay leaves in a 6-quart soup pot with 6 cups cold water over medium-high heat. When the water begins to boil, lower the heat and simmer about 45 minutes, until the lentils are tender. Season with salt to taste.

Meanwhile, heat the oil in a medium skillet over medium heat. Add the garlic, peperoncino, and oyster mushrooms. Season with salt and pepper. Gently cook, stirring, about 10 minutes, until lightly browned.

Ladle the lentil soup into bowls and top each serving with oyster mushrooms.

MAKES 6 SERVINGS

SOUP OF LENTILS AND CHESTNUTS

I first sampled this delicious soup in an old trattoria in Naples called Amici Mei. It's surprisingly simple, and it has a great taste and marvelous texture from the chestnuts. While you can prepare this soup with canned chestnuts, both the flavor and the consistency are superior when you use fresh ones. Shelling them is much easier than it may appear. The shells can easily be cut with a sharp knife, and once cut, the shells readily peel away. Occasionally, the inner layer of shell covering adheres to the chestnuts. You can easily peel it off with a paring knife. Serve this soup as they did in the trattoria, with crusty toast broken into pieces and dropped into the soup.

¼	CUP OLIVE OIL
1	SMALL RED ONION, FINELY CHOPPED
1	RIB CELERY, FINELY CHOPPED
3	LEAVES FRESH BASIL, FINELY CHOPPED
¼	TEASPOON FINELY CHOPPED FRESH THYME
1	BAY LEAF
1	CUP SHELLED FRESH CHESTNUT PIECES
1	CUP ITALIAN SMALL BROWN LENTILS OR FRENCH GREEN LENTILS
1	TABLESPOON TOMATO PASTE
	SALT AND FRESHLY GROUND BLACK PEPPER
6	SLICES (1 INCH EACH) CRUSTY RUSTIC COUNTRY BREAD, TOASTED

Heat the olive oil in a heavy 6-quart soup pot or casserole over medium heat. Add the onion, celery, basil, and thyme and cook, stirring, about 3 minutes, until the onion begins to soften. Add the bay leaf, chestnuts, and lentils. Dissolve the tomato paste in 6 cups cold water and stir into the pot. Raise the heat to medium-high. When the soup begins to boil, lower the heat and simmer, partially covered, about 45 minutes, until the lentils are tender. Remove and discard the bay leaf.

Transfer about half of the soup to a food processor or blender, or use an immersion hand blender, and process until smooth. Add it back to the soup pot. Season with salt and pepper to taste and reheat before serving.

Toast the bread until lightly browned. Serve the soup with the toast.

MAKES 6 SERVINGS

CHICKPEA AND FARRO SOUP

This soup is from Umbria, the region that sits just to the east of Tuscany. Some of Italy's best food products come from there, including black truffles. It is also known for its delicious farro *(whole wheat) and wonderful beans.*

1	CUP CHICKPEAS
2	BAY LEAVES
2	STEMS FRESH ROSEMARY, LEAVES ONLY, CHOPPED
½	CUP FARRO (SEE INGREDIENT GUIDE ON PAGE 19)
⅓	CUP OLIVE OIL, PLUS MORE FOR SERVING
1	SMALL RED ONION, FINELY CHOPPED
1	CARROT, FINELY CHOPPED
1	RIB CELERY, FINELY CHOPPED
2	CLOVES GARLIC, PEELED AND FINELY CHOPPED
8	STEMS FRESH ITALIAN FLAT-LEAF PARSLEY, LEAVES ONLY, CHOPPED
1	TABLESPOON TOMATO PASTE
	SALT AND FRESHLY GROUND BLACK PEPPER

Soak the chickpeas in cold water for 8 hours or longer. Drain and discard the soaking water. Rinse under cold water and drain again.

Combine the chickpeas with the bay leaves, half of the rosemary, and 10 cups cold water in a heavy 6-quart soup pot or casserole over medium-high heat. When the water begins to boil, lower the heat and simmer, uncovered, for 1 to 1½ hours, until the chickpeas are tender. Remove and discard the bay leaves. Transfer about 2 cups of the chickpeas and some of the cooking liquid to a food processor or blender and process until smooth. Add back to the pot.

Meanwhile, soak the farro in cold water for 45 minutes. Drain and discard the soaking water.

Heat the olive oil in a small skillet over medium heat. Add the onion, carrot, celery, garlic, remaining rosemary, the parsley, and tomato paste and cook, stirring frequently, 5 to 7 minutes, until the onion is translucent and the vegetables are soft. Add the vegetables and the farro to the chickpeas. Raise the heat to medium-high, and when the soup begins to boil, lower the heat and simmer, uncovered, about 40 minutes, until the farro is tender and the soup is thick. Season with salt and pepper to taste.

Serve in individual soup bowls with a drizzle of olive oil on each serving.

MAKES 6 SERVINGS

Zuppa di fagioli e farro

SOUP OF CANNELLINI AND FARRO

This soup is from Florence. It is prepared with cannellini and farro, the deliciously nutty-tasting whole wheat from Tuscany, Umbria, and the Marches. You can make this soup a day ahead of time and reheat it when you are ready to serve.

1   CUP DRIED CANNELLINI OR GREAT NORTHERN BEANS

½   CUP CANNED CHOPPED TOMATOES, WITH THEIR JUICE

2   STEMS FRESH ROSEMARY

2   LARGE CLOVES GARLIC, PEELED, 1 WHOLE, 1 FINELY CHOPPED

SALT AND FRESHLY GROUND BLACK PEPPER

½   CUP FARRO (SEE INGREDIENT GUIDE ON PAGE 19)

⅓   CUP OLIVE OIL, PLUS MORE FOR SERVING

1   SMALL RED ONION, FINELY CHOPPED

1   RIB CELERY, FINELY CHOPPED

6   LEAVES FRESH SAGE, FINELY CHOPPED

Soak the beans in cold water for 8 hours or longer. Drain and discard the soaking water. Rinse under cold water and drain again. Combine the beans, tomatoes, rosemary, and the whole clove of garlic with 8 cups cold water in a heavy 6-quart soup pot or casserole over medium-high heat. When the water begins to boil, lower the heat and simmer, uncovered, stirring occasionally, about 1 hour, until the beans are tender. Remove and discard the rosemary stems. Transfer 1 cup of the beans and some of the cooking liquid to a food processor or blender. Process until smooth and return to the pot. Season with salt and pepper to taste.

Meanwhile, soak the farro in cold water for 45 minutes. Drain and discard the soaking water.

Heat the olive oil in a small skillet over medium-high heat. Add the chopped garlic, onion, celery, and sage and cook, stirring, 2 to 3 minutes, until the vegetables begin to soften. Add them to the pot with the beans and bring the liquid to a simmer. Stir in the farro and continue cooking, stirring frequently, about 45 minutes, until the farro is tender and the soup is thick. Add a drizzle of olive oil to each serving.

MAKES 6 SERVINGS

Zuppa di cereali e fagioli

SOUP OF FARRO, BARLEY, CHICKPEAS, AND BORLOTTI

In the Piemonte hill town of Bra, the Ascheri family has been producing wines since the 1880s. They also run the wonderful Osteria Murivecchi, which fills the space of their old original wine cellar. This rustic, informal restaurant has exposed brick walls and comfortable antique wooden tables and chairs. The food there, like this soup, is simple, traditional, and very good.

1	CUP CHICKPEAS
1	CUP DRIED BORLOTTI, PINTO, OR CRANBERRY BEANS
⅔	CUP FARRO (SEE INGREDIENT GUIDE ON PAGE 19)
⅔	CUP PEARL BARLEY
6	OUNCES PROSCIUTTO (SEE INGREDIENT GUIDE ON PAGE 19), DICED
2	TABLESPOONS OLIVE OIL, PLUS MORE FOR SERVING
1	RED ONION, CHOPPED
8	STEMS FRESH ITALIAN FLAT-LEAF PARSLEY, LEAVES ONLY, CHOPPED
1	TABLESPOON TOMATO PASTE
2	MEDIUM YUKON GOLD OR YELLOW FINN POTATOES, PEELED AND FINELY SLICED
	SALT AND FRESHLY GROUND BLACK PEPPER

Soak the chickpeas, beans, farro, and barley in cold water for 8 hours or longer. Drain and discard the soaking water. Rinse under cold water and drain again.

Transfer the beans and grains to a heavy 6-quart soup pot or casserole. Add 10 cups cold water and place over medium-high heat. When the water begins to boil, lower the heat and simmer, uncovered, about 1 hour, until the beans are tender.

Meanwhile, combine the prosciutto with the olive oil in a medium skillet over medium-high heat. Cook about 10 minutes, until the prosciutto begins to turn brown. Add the onion and parsley and continue cooking 2 to 3 minutes longer, until the onion begins to soften. Add the tomato paste, stir until it dissolves, and add to the pot with the beans and grains. Add the potatoes and continue cooking, 30 to 45 minutes longer, until the potatoes are falling-apart tender and the soup is thick. Season with salt and pepper to taste. Add a drizzle of olive oil to each serving.

MAKES 6 SERVINGS

Zuppa di fave e farro

SOUP OF FAVA BEANS AND FARRO

In this soup from Umbria, the favas are harmoniously paired with farro *and carrots.*

1	CUP DRIED SPLIT, SKINNED FAVA BEANS
¾	CUP FARRO (SEE INGREDIENT GUIDE ON PAGE 19)
¼	CUP OLIVE OIL
2	CARROTS, THINLY SLICED INTO ROUNDS
½	RED ONION, CHOPPED
¼	CUP CANNED CHOPPED TOMATOES, WITH THEIR JUICE
	SALT AND FRESHLY GROUND BLACK PEPPER
8	LEAVES FRESH BASIL, TORN INTO SMALL PIECES
	EXTRA VIRGIN OLIVE OIL, FOR SERVING
	GRATED AGED PECORINO TOSCANO CHEESE, FOR SERVING

Soak the favas and farro in cold water for 1 hour. Drain, rinse under cold water, and drain again.

Heat the olive oil in a heavy 6-quart soup pot or casserole over medium heat. Add the carrots and onion and cook about 3 minutes, until the onion begins to soften. Add 8 cups cold water, the fava beans and farro, and the tomatoes with their juice. When the water begins to boil, lower the heat and simmer, partially covered, about 1 hour, until the soup is thick and the fava beans are tender. Season with salt and pepper to taste. Stir in the basil leaves.

Ladle the soup into bowls and add a drizzle of extra virgin olive oil and some of the pecorino toscano cheese to each serving.

MAKES 6 SERVINGS

Mes-ciua

LIGURIAN SOUP OF CHICKPEAS, CANNELLINI, AND FARRO

Pronounced "meh-SHOO-ah," this traditional Ligurian bean soup is a simple combination of chickpeas, cannellini, and whole wheat (farro). It's more porridge than soup. There is no broth and no vegetables. When the soup is finished, it's seasoned with lots of black pepper and dressed with really good olive oil.

1½   CUPS CHICKPEAS
1½   CUPS DRIED CANNELLINI OR GREAT NORTHERN
       BEANS
½   CUP FARRO (SEE INGREDIENT GUIDE ON PAGE 19)
       SALT
1   TEASPOON FRESHLY GROUND BLACK PEPPER,
       OR MORE TO TASTE
       OLIVE OIL, FOR SERVING

Soak the chickpeas, beans, and farro in cold water for 8 hours or longer. Drain and discard the soaking water. Rinse under cold water and drain again.

Transfer to a heavy 6-quart soup pot or casserole with 10 cups cold water and place over medium-high heat. When the water begins to boil, lower the heat and simmer, partially covered, stirring occasionally, about 2 hours, until the beans and farro are tender and the soup is thick. Season with salt to taste and stir in the pepper.

Serve with a generous drizzle of olive oil on each serving.

MAKES 6 SERVINGS

TUSCAN CANNELLINI, BORLOTTI, AND FARRO SOUP

The Garfagnana is an area just beyond the old walled city of Lucca, in Tuscany, where farro, a type of whole wheat that is also called spelt, is cultivated. Since I encountered this soup there, I have been preparing it at home regularly.

¾ CUP DRIED CANNELLINI, SORANINI, OR GREAT NORTHERN BEANS

½ CUP DRIED BORLOTTI, PINTO, OR CRANBERRY BEANS

¾ CUP FARRO (SEE INGREDIENT GUIDE ON PAGE 19)

2 TABLESPOONS OLIVE OIL, PLUS MORE FOR SERVING

4 OUNCES PANCETTA (SEE INGREDIENT GUIDE ON PAGE 19), CUT INTO SMALL DICE

1 MEDIUM RED ONION, FINELY CHOPPED

1 MEDIUM CARROT, FINELY CHOPPED

1 RIB CELERY, FINELY CHOPPED

1 LARGE CLOVE GARLIC, PEELED AND FINELY CHOPPED

4 LEAVES FRESH SAGE, CHOPPED

SALT AND FRESHLY GROUND BLACK PEPPER

Soak the beans and farro together in cold water for 8 hours or longer. Drain and discard the soaking water. Rinse under cold water and drain again.

In a heavy 6-quart soup pot or casserole, combine the olive oil and pancetta and place over medium-low heat. Cook, stirring, about 10 minutes, until the pancetta begins to brown. Stir in the onion, carrot, celery, and garlic and continue cooking, 3 to 5 minutes longer, until the vegetables begin to soften. Add the bean and farro mixture, 8 cups cold water, and sage and raise the heat to medium-high. When the water begins to boil, lower the heat and simmer, partially covered, stirring occasionally, about 1 hour, until the beans and farro are tender and the soup is thick.

Transfer about 1 cup of the soup to a blender or food processor. Process until smooth and return to the pot. Season with salt and pepper to taste and continue cooking, about 15 minutes longer.

Add a generous drizzle of olive oil to each serving.

MAKES 6 SERVINGS

Zuppa di orzo e fagioli

BORLOTTI AND BARLEY SOUP FROM THE VENETO

Borlotti *bean and barley soup is traditional in the northern Italian regions of the Veneto and Friuli. It is served everywhere. This recipe comes from an extraordinary restaurant, Antica Trattoria Boschetti, in Tricesimo, near Udine.*

2   CUPS DRIED BORLOTTI, PINTO, OR CRANBERRY
    BEANS

¼   CUP PEARL BARLEY

1   TABLESPOON OLIVE OIL, PLUS MORE FOR SERVING

3   OUNCES SMOKED OR PLAIN PANCETTA
    (SEE INGREDIENT GUIDE ON PAGE 19), DICED

1   MEDIUM YELLOW ONION, FINELY CHOPPED

1   MEDIUM CARROT, CHOPPED

1   MEDIUM YUKON GOLD OR YELLOW FINN POTATO,
    PEELED AND DICED

1   RIB CELERY, FINELY CHOPPED

1   CLOVE GARLIC, PEELED AND FINELY CHOPPED

1   LARGE LEAF FRESH SAGE, FINELY CHOPPED

8   STEMS FRESH ITALIAN FLAT-LEAF PARSLEY,
    LEAVES ONLY, CHOPPED

1   STEM FRESH ROSEMARY, LEAVES ONLY, CHOPPED

3   LARGE LEAVES FRESH BASIL, CHOPPED

1   BAY LEAF

    SALT AND FRESHLY GROUND BLACK PEPPER

Soak the beans in cold water for 8 hours or longer. Drain and discard the soaking water. Rinse under cold water and drain again.

Combine the barley with 4 cups cold water in a small saucepan over medium-high heat. When the water begins to boil, lower the heat and simmer, uncovered, about 45 minutes, until the barley is tender. Drain and set aside.

Combine the olive oil and pancetta in a heavy 6-quart soup pot or casserole over medium heat. Cook, stirring frequently, until the pancetta renders most of its fat and begins to brown, about 10 minutes. Stir in the onion, carrot, potato, celery, and garlic and cook about 3 minutes longer, until the vegetables begin to soften. Add the beans, sage, 1 tablespoon of the parsley, the rosemary, basil, and bay leaf.

Add 8 cups cold water and raise the heat to medium-high. When the water begins to boil, lower the heat and simmer, partially covered, stirring occasionally, about 1 hour, until the beans are tender. Discard the bay leaf.

Transfer about half the soup to a food processor or blender, or use an immersion hand blender, and process until smooth. Return the soup to the pot, season with salt and pepper to taste, and add the cooked barley. Place the soup over medium heat, bring to a simmer, and cook 15 minutes, stirring frequently to prevent the barley from sticking to the bottom of the pot.

Add a drizzle of olive oil and a sprinkling of the remaining chopped parsley to each serving.

MAKES 6 SERVINGS

Zuppa di orzo perlato e fave

FAVA BEAN AND BARLEY SOUP

Umbria is one of the richest bean- and grain-growing regions of Italy. This recipe from Assisi is made with fava beans and pearl barley. When cooked, the dried fava beans become luxuriously creamy.

1½ CUPS DRIED SPLIT, SKINNED FAVA BEANS

⅓ CUP PEARL BARLEY

¼ CUP OLIVE OIL

1 CLOVE GARLIC, PEELED AND FINELY CHOPPED

1 MEDIUM RED ONION, CHOPPED

8 CUPS CHICKEN OR VEGETABLE BROTH

SALT AND FRESHLY GROUND BLACK PEPPER

15 STEMS FRESH ITALIAN FLAT-LEAF PARSLEY, LEAVES ONLY, FINELY CHOPPED

½ CUP GRATED PARMIGIANO CHEESE

EXTRA VIRGIN OLIVE OIL, FOR SERVING

Soak the fava beans and barley in separate bowls with cold water to cover for 1 hour. Drain separately. Discard the soaking water and rinse under cold water. Drain again.

Heat the olive oil in a heavy 6-quart soup pot or casserole over medium heat. Add the garlic and onion and cook, stirring, about 5 minutes, until the onion is soft. Add the fava beans and broth and bring to a boil. Lower the heat and simmer, uncovered, stirring occasionally, about 45 minutes, until the soup is creamy. The beans will fall apart. Season with salt and pepper to taste. Stir in the barley and continue cooking about 40 minutes, until it is tender.

When the soup is done, add the parsley and parmigiano cheese and stir well to combine. Add a drizzle of extra virgin olive oil to each serving.

MAKES 6 SERVINGS

Crema di ceci

CREAMY CHICKPEA SOUP
WITH ROSEMARY AND GARLIC

Chickpeas become deliciously smooth and creamy when pureed, making this a very richly textured soup. The olive oil, infused with rosemary, garlic, and lots of freshly ground black pepper, adds a lot of flavor.

2	CUPS CHICKPEAS
3	CLOVES GARLIC, PEELED
2	STEMS FRESH ROSEMARY
6	TABLESPOONS OLIVE OIL
	SALT AND FRESHLY GROUND BLACK PEPPER

Soak the chickpeas in cold water for 8 hours or longer. Drain and discard the soaking water. Rinse under cold water and drain again. Combine the beans in a heavy 6-quart soup pot or casserole with 1 clove of the garlic, 1 rosemary stem, 3 tablespoons olive oil, and 8 to 10 cups cold water over high heat. When the water begins to boil, lower the heat and simmer, uncovered, about 1½ hours, until the chickpeas are soft. Drain and reserve the cooking water.

Transfer the chickpeas to a food processor or blender, process until smooth, and return to the pot. Add enough of the cooking liquid to the puree to make a smooth, creamy consistency. Season with salt and pepper to taste and reheat before serving.

Meanwhile, heat the remaining 3 tablespoons olive oil with the remaining garlic and rosemary in a small saucepan over medium-low heat, being careful not to burn them. After 10 minutes, turn off the heat, remove the garlic and rosemary, and set the olive oil aside.

When you are ready to serve, ladle the soup into bowls and drizzle with the flavored olive oil.

MAKES 6 SERVINGS

CREAMY CANNELLINI
AND ASPARAGUS SOUP

In Umbria, this rich and flavorful soup is served in the early spring, when fresh asparagus is plentiful in the markets. To remove any traces of the vegetables' fibrous skin and to ensure a smooth, creamy consistency, the asparagus spears should be peeled before cooking. You can use an ordinary vegetable peeler.

1   CUP DRIED CANNELLINI OR GREAT NORTHERN BEANS

5   TABLESPOONS OLIVE OIL, PLUS MORE FOR SERVING

½   CUP CHOPPED SHALLOTS OR FINELY CHOPPED RED ONION

1   RIB CELERY, FINELY CHOPPED

1   CLOVE GARLIC, PEELED AND FINELY CHOPPED

2   OUNCES PROSCIUTTO (SEE INGREDIENT GUIDE ON PAGE 19), DICED

1   MEDIUM YUKON GOLD OR YELLOW FINN POTATO, PEELED AND THINLY SLICED

½   CUP TOMATO PUREE

1   POUND FRESH ASPARAGUS, BOTTOM 2 INCHES CUT OFF AND DISCARDED, SPEARS PEELED

     SALT AND FRESHLY GROUND WHITE PEPPER

Soak the beans in cold water for 8 hours or longer. Drain and discard the soaking water. Rinse under cold water and drain again. Put the beans in a medium saucepan with 6 cups cold water and place over medium-high heat. When the water begins to boil, lower the heat and simmer, about 1 hour, until the beans are tender. Drain and reserve the cooking liquid.

Meanwhile, heat the olive oil in a heavy 6-quart soup pot or casserole over medium heat. Add the shallots or onion, celery, garlic, and prosciutto and cook, stirring, about 5 minutes, until the vegetables begin to soften and the pro-sciutto loses its raw color. Add the potato, tomato puree, asparagus, and beans. Stir in 4 cups of the reserved bean broth and simmer the soup, stirring occasionally, about 30 minutes, until the asparagus and potatoes are tender. Transfer the soup to a blender or food processor, or use an immersion hand blender, and process until smooth. The soup will retain some texture from the pieces of prosciutto. Return the soup to the pot, season with salt and pepper to taste, and reheat before serving.

Add a drizzle of olive oil to each serving.

MAKES 6 SERVINGS

VENETO-STYLE SOUP OF BORLOTTI AND VEGETABLES

A creamy puree of borlotti beans and vegetables with a hint of sweetness makes this soup rich and flavorful. You can omit the prosciutto from the recipe and use chicken or vegetable broth in place of the water.

1   CUP DRIED BORLOTTI, PINTO, OR CRANBERRY BEANS

1   MEDIUM RED ONION, COARSELY CHOPPED

1   MEDIUM CARROT, CHOPPED

3   RIBS CELERY, CHOPPED

1   CLOVE GARLIC, PEELED AND FINELY CHOPPED

1   LEEK, WHITE PART ONLY, TRIMMED, RINSED, AND SLICED

3   LARGE LEAVES FRESH SAGE

2   OUNCES PROSCIUTTO (SEE INGREDIENT GUIDE ON PAGE 19), IN ONE PIECE

SALT AND FRESHLY GROUND BLACK PEPPER

OLIVE OIL, FOR SERVING

Soak the beans in cold water for 8 hours or longer. Drain and discard the soaking water. Rinse under cold water and drain again. Combine the beans with the onion, carrot, celery, garlic, leek, sage, prosciutto, and 6 cups cold water in a heavy 6-quart soup pot or casserole over medium-high heat. When the water begins to boil, lower the heat and simmer, uncovered, about 1½ hours, until the beans are tender. Remove the piece of prosciutto and reserve to eat separately.

Drain the beans and vegetables, reserving the cooking liquid, and transfer to a food processor or blender. Process until almost smooth. I like this soup to retain some texture. Return the puree to the pot and add enough of the cooking liquid, about 1 cup, to give the soup a creamy consistency. Season with salt and pepper to taste. Reheat before serving. Add a drizzle of olive oil to each serving.

MAKES 6 SERVINGS

CREAMY FAVA BEAN AND FRESH FENNEL SOUP

The fava beans give this soup a luxurious texture. The original recipe, from Umbria, calls for smoked ricotta to be grated on each serving. You can also use ricotta salata, which is more readily available in the United States. The ricotta isn't a hard cheese, but it's firm enough to grate.

2   CUPS DRIED SPLIT, SKINNED FAVA BEANS

1   BULB FRESH FENNEL, INCLUDING TOPS AND FRONDS, CUT INTO 2-INCH PIECES

2   CLOVES GARLIC, PEELED AND SLICED

3   TABLESPOONS OLIVE OIL, PLUS MORE FOR SERVING

2   TEASPOONS DRIED FENNEL SEED, PULVERIZED (ABOUT 1 TEASPOON POWDERED)

    SALT AND FRESHLY GROUND BLACK PEPPER

4   OUNCES RICOTTA SALATA CHEESE, GRATED

Combine the beans with the fresh fennel, garlic, and olive oil in a heavy 6-quart soup pot or casserole. Add 8 cups cold water and place over medium-high heat. When the water begins to boil, lower the heat and simmer about 45 minutes, until the favas are tender and falling apart.

Transfer the soup to a food processor or blender, or use an immersion hand blender, and process until smooth. The soup should be thick, with the consistency of heavy cream. Add more water to the soup if it seems too thick. Return the soup to the pot, add ½ teaspoon of the fennel seed powder and salt and pepper to taste, and stir well to combine. Place over medium-low heat and gently reheat before serving.

To serve, dust the remaining fennel seed powder over each serving, add a drizzle of olive oil, and top with some of the grated cheese.

MAKES 6 SERVINGS

CREAMY SOUP OF FAVA BEANS AND ARTICHOKES

This is a delectable soup from the Pugliese city of Lecce, in the heel of Italy's boot. Although the soup is pureed, it will retain some texture from the artichokes. Strain it through a sieve before serving if you want an ultra-smooth soup.

¼	CUP OLIVE OIL
1	MEDIUM RED OR WHITE ONION, CHOPPED
1	RIB CELERY, FINELY CHOPPED
1	CLOVE GARLIC, PEELED AND FINELY CHOPPED
8	STEMS FRESH ITALIAN FLAT-LEAF PARSLEY, LEAVES ONLY, CHOPPED
4	MEDIUM ARTICHOKES, LEAVES PEELED AND TRIMMED DOWN TO THE HEART, CHOKE REMOVED, THINLY SLICED
1	CUP DRIED SPLIT, SKINNED FAVA BEANS
	SALT AND FRESHLY GROUND BLACK PEPPER

Heat the olive oil in a heavy 6-quart soup pot or casserole over medium-high heat. Add the onion, celery, garlic, and parsley and cook, stirring, about 3 minutes, until the onion begins to soften. Stir in the artichokes and continue cooking about 3 minutes longer. Add the beans and 8 cups cold water. Bring the liquid to a boil. Lower the heat and simmer, partially covered, about 1 hour, until the beans are soft. Season with salt and pepper to taste and continue cooking 10 minutes longer.

Transfer the soup to a food processor or blender, or use an immersion hand blender, and process until the beans and vegetables are smooth. Return the puree to the pot. Reheat before serving.

MAKES 6 SERVINGS

PASTA AND BEANS

There are probably as many recipes for *pasta e fagioli* as there are cooks in Italy. *Pasta e fagioli* encompasses a wide range of preparations for beans and pasta. In the north of Italy, it is usually a soup, while in the south (in Campania, Puglia, and Calabria), *pasta e fagioli* is often a thick mixture of pasta and beans—more of a pasta with bean sauce than a soup. Another distinction is how the pasta is cooked. In *pasta e fagioli* soups, the pasta is typically cooked in the soup, while in *pasta e fagioli* pasta dishes, the pasta is first cooked in boiling water and then added to the beans.

When choosing pasta for bean dishes, shorter shapes, including *ditalini, tubetti* (short macaroni), and *conchigliette* (small shells), are generally best. Long pasta strands such as *tagliatelle, spaghetti, linguine,* and *fettuccine* are also common in *pasta e fagioli,* but they're always broken into smaller pieces before they're added to the soup. As a rule, I break the strands in thirds. In southern Italy, *pasta e fagioli* is often prepared with a *mischiata,* a mix, of pasta shapes. This is traditionally a way to use up the odds and ends of pasta that accumulate over the course of a week or two. I find that a combination of pasta shapes adds interesting texture to a dish, but I also have a sentimental fondness for it. It reminds me of the pasta my grandmother and I would cook together when I was young. We would go through the cupboard, take noodles from every box, and cook them all together. We'd finish the dish with lots of butter and cheese.

You can prepare any of the dishes in this chapter ahead of time, but always add and cook the pasta just before you plan to serve it. If the cooked pasta stands, it absorbs most of the liquid in the dish. The pasta becomes too soft and the dish too dry. You know the pasta is done when it is *al dente:* tender but firm—never crunchy—to the bite.

When figuring quantities, all of these pasta dishes will generously serve four people as a main course and six as a first course.

Pasta e fagioli alla fiorentina

FLORENTINE SOUP OF PASTA AND CANNELLINI

This is a simple bean and pasta soup from Florence, where cannellini are traditionally cooked with just about anything and everything. This soup offers many of the flavors you'll find in Tuscany, including garlic, rosemary, and hot pepper.

1	CUP DRIED CANNELLINI OR GREAT NORTHERN BEANS
6	CLOVES GARLIC, PEELED, 3 WHOLE, 3 FINELY CHOPPED
2	STEMS FRESH ROSEMARY, LEAVES ONLY, CHOPPED
8	LEAVES FRESH SAGE, FINELY CHOPPED
½	CUP OLIVE OIL
	PINCH OF PEPERONCINO (RED PEPPER FLAKES)
	SALT
1	CUP DRIED DITALINI, OR OTHER SMALL TUBULAR PASTA

Soak the beans in cold water for 8 hours or longer. Drain and discard the soaking water. Rinse under cold water and drain again. Combine the beans with the 3 whole cloves of garlic, half of the rosemary, half of the sage, and 10 cups cold water in a heavy 6-quart soup pot or casserole over medium-high heat. When the water boils, lower the heat and simmer, partially covered, about 1 hour, until the beans are tender.

Heat ¼ cup olive oil in a small saucepan over medium heat. Add the chopped garlic and peperoncino and cook, gently, 2 to 3 minutes, being careful not to brown the garlic.

Add to the soup and simmer, about 5 minutes. Season with salt to taste. Add the pasta and continue cooking, stirring frequently to prevent the pasta from sticking to the bottom of the pot, 10 to 12 minutes longer, until the pasta is tender but firm to the bite, al dente.

Meanwhile, heat the remaining ¼ cup olive oil with the remaining rosemary and sage over low heat. When the soup is finished, add the oil and herb mixture and stir well to combine before serving.

MAKES 4 SERVINGS

SIGNORA PISTELLI'S SOUP OF PURGATORIO BEANS AND PASTA

Enzo Pistelli is a bean grower in Terni, in southern Umbria. His mother, who lives with him and his family, prepares this simple soup of the small white beans, called fagioli del purgatorio *in Umbria, that Pistelli grows in his fields. Purgatorio beans require less soaking than most other beans because of their small size. Navy beans are a good substitute.*

1   CUP DRIED FAGIOLI DEL PURGATORIO OR NAVY BEANS
1   CLOVE GARLIC, PEELED AND FINELY CHOPPED
3   LARGE LEAVES FRESH SAGE, CHOPPED
½   CUP CANNED CHOPPED TOMATOES, WITH THEIR JUICE, OR TOMATO PUREE
    SALT
1   CUP DRIED CONCHIGLIETTE (SMALL SHELLS)
    OLIVE OIL

Soak the beans in cold water for 4 hours. Drain and discard the soaking water. Rinse under cold water and drain again.

Combine the beans with the garlic, sage, tomatoes, and 8 cups cold water in a heavy medium saucepan over medium-high heat. When the water begins to boil, lower the heat and simmer, uncovered, 40 to 45 minutes, until the beans are tender. Season with salt to taste and add the pasta. Raise the heat to medium-high and cook, stirring frequently to prevent the pasta from sticking to the bottom of the pot, 10 to 12 minutes, until the pasta is tender but firm to the bite, al dente. Add a drizzle of good olive oil to each serving.

MAKES 4 SERVINGS

Zuppa di pasta e ceci

SOUP OF PASTA AND CHICKPEAS

Chickpeas are found all over Italy, but this soup is typically Tuscan. It's one of my favorites. The best pasta for this soup is very short macaroni called ditalini *or* tubetti. *As with all* pasta e fagioli, *serve this soup as soon as the pasta is done.*

1 CUP CHICKPEAS
5 TABLESPOONS OLIVE OIL, PLUS MORE FOR SERVING
1 LARGE CLOVE GARLIC, PEELED
1 STEM FRESH ROSEMARY, LEAVES ONLY, CHOPPED
1 CUP CANNED CHOPPED TOMATOES, WITH THEIR JUICE
6 OUNCES DRIED SHORT PASTA, SUCH AS DITALINI
   OR TUBETTI
   SALT AND FRESHLY GROUND BLACK PEPPER

Soak the chickpeas in cold water for 8 hours or longer. Drain and discard the soaking water, rinse under cold water, and drain again.

Combine the beans with the olive oil, garlic, rosemary, and tomatoes in a heavy 6-quart soup pot or casserole with 10 cups cold water over medium-high heat. When the water begins to boil, lower the heat and simmer, uncovered, about 2 hours, until the chickpeas are tender. Pass half of the chickpeas through a food mill or puree in a food processor or blender, and return them to the soup. Add the pasta and continue cooking, stirring frequently to prevent the pasta from sticking to the bottom of the pot, 10 to 12 minutes, until the pasta is tender but firm to the bite, al dente. Season with salt and pepper to taste. Add a drizzle of olive oil to each serving.

MAKES 6 SERVINGS

VENETO-STYLE SOUP OF PASTA AND BORLOTTI

This is a traditional recipe from the town of Lamon in Veneto, the region to the northwest of Venice. Lamon sits in the foothills of the Dolomites, the Italian Alps. This dish is typically prepared with locally grown fagioli di Lamon—beans more easily obtained, like the pinto or cranberry bean, can be used—and tagliatelle egg pasta.

1	CUP DRIED FAGIOLI DI LAMON, BORLOTTI, PINTO, OR CRANBERRY BEANS
4	OUNCES PROSCIUTTO (SEE INGREDIENT GUIDE ON PAGE 19), CHOPPED
3	TABLESPOONS OLIVE OIL, PLUS MORE FOR SERVING
1	MEDIUM CARROT, CHOPPED
1	MEDIUM RED ONION, CHOPPED
1	RIB CELERY, CHOPPED
	SALT AND FRESHLY GROUND BLACK PEPPER
4	OUNCES DRIED TAGLIATELLE OR FETTUCCINE EGG PASTA, BROKEN UP

Soak the beans in cold water for 8 hours or longer. Drain and discard the soaking water. Rinse under cold water and drain again. Combine the beans with the prosciutto and 10 cups cold water in a heavy 6-quart soup pot or casserole over high heat. When the water begins to boil, lower the heat and simmer, uncovered, about 1½ hours, until the beans are tender.

Meanwhile, heat the olive oil in a small skillet over medium heat. Add the carrot, onion, and celery and cook, stirring frequently, 7 to 10 minutes, until the onion is translucent. Add to the pot with the beans and continue cooking, stirring occasionally.

When the beans are very tender, transfer the soup to a blender or food processor, or use a food mill or immersion hand blender, and process until almost smooth. It's all right to have some texture in the soup. Return it to the pot and season with salt and pepper to taste. Bring the soup back to a boil, add the pasta, and cook, stirring frequently to prevent the pasta from sticking to the bottom of the pot, 10 to 12 minutes, until the pasta is tender but firm to the bite, al dente. Add a drizzle of olive oil to each serving.

MAKES 6 SERVINGS

SOUP OF PASTA, CANNELLINI, AND POTATO

Pasta, potatoes, and beans are a common trio of ingredients in soups in many parts of Italy. This recipe comes from Tuscany. It is a harmonious combination, and you'll find this soup surprisingly light.

1½ CUPS DRIED CANNELLINI OR GREAT NORTHERN BEANS

2 BAY LEAVES

2 TABLESPOONS OLIVE OIL, PLUS MORE FOR SERVING

2 OUNCES PANCETTA (SEE INGREDIENT GUIDE ON PAGE 19), CUT INTO SMALL DICE

2 YUKON GOLD OR YELLOW FINN POTATOES, PEELED AND COARSELY CHOPPED

1 RIB CELERY, FINELY CHOPPED

½ CUP CANNED CHOPPED TOMATOES, WITH THEIR JUICE

6 CUPS CHICKEN OR VEGETABLE BROTH

8 STEMS FRESH ITALIAN FLAT-LEAF PARSLEY, LEAVES ONLY, CHOPPED

SALT AND FRESHLY GROUND BLACK PEPPER

1 CUP DRIED SMALL TUBULAR PASTA, SUCH AS DITALINI OR TUBETTI

Soak the beans in cold water for 8 hours or longer. Drain and discard the soaking water. Rinse under cold water and drain again. Combine the beans with the bay leaves and 6 cups cold water in a heavy medium saucepan over medium-high heat. When the water begins to boil, lower the heat and simmer, uncovered, about 1 hour, or until the beans are tender. Drain and discard the bay leaves. Set aside.

Heat the olive oil in a heavy 6-quart soup pot or casserole over medium-low heat. Add the pancetta and cook slowly, about 10 minutes, until the pancetta is brown. Stir in the potatoes, celery, tomatoes, beans, broth, and parsley. Raise the heat to medium-high and bring the broth to a boil. Lower the heat and simmer, uncovered, 45 minutes. Season with salt and pepper to taste. Add the pasta and continue cooking, stirring frequently to prevent the pasta from sticking to the bottom of the pot, 10 to 12 minutes longer, until the pasta is tender but firm to the bite, al dente.

Add a drizzle of olive oil to each serving.

MAKES 6 SERVINGS

PASTA AND CANNELLINI SOUP
PISA-STYLE

This sumptuous pasta and bean soup from the Leaning Tower city of Pisa is one you might encounter anywhere in Tuscany, as the ingredients are typical of Tuscan cooking. Be sure to use a small pasta shape; it gives the soup a pleasing texture.

2 CUPS DRIED CANNELLINI OR GREAT NORTHERN BEANS

3 CLOVES GARLIC, PEELED

9 LEAVES FRESH SAGE

5 TABLESPOONS OLIVE OIL, PLUS MORE FOR SERVING

1 MEDIUM RED ONION, FINELY CHOPPED

1 RIB CELERY, FINELY CHOPPED

1 CUP CANNED CHOPPED TOMATOES, WITH THEIR JUICE

SALT AND FRESHLY GROUND BLACK PEPPER

1 CUP DRIED SMALL TUBULAR PASTA SUCH AS TUBETTI OR DITALINI

Soak the beans in cold water for 8 hours or longer. Drain and discard the soaking water. Rinse under cold water and drain again. Combine the beans with 1 whole clove of garlic, 3 sage leaves, 2 tablespoons olive oil, and 8 cups cold water in a heavy 6-quart soup pot or casserole over medium-high heat. When the water begins to boil, lower the heat and simmer, uncovered, about 1 hour, until the beans are tender.

Meanwhile, finely chop together the onion, celery, the remaining 2 cloves of garlic, and the remaining 6 sage leaves. Heat the remaining 3 tablespoons olive oil in a small skillet over medium heat. Add the chopped vegetables and cook, stirring, about 3 minutes, until the onion and celery begin to soften. Turn off the heat and set aside.

When the beans are tender, discard the garlic and sage they were cooked with. Add the sauteed vegetables to the beans along with the chopped tomatoes and bring the soup back to a low simmer. Cook 30 minutes. Season with salt and pepper to taste. Add the pasta and continue cooking, stirring frequently to prevent the pasta from sticking to the bottom of the pot, 10 to 12 minutes longer, until the pasta is tender but firm to the bite, al dente. Add a drizzle of olive oil to each serving.

MAKES 6 SERVINGS

SOUP OF PASTA, BORLOTTI, LENTILS, AND SPLIT PEAS

This Tuscan soup makes a satisfying meal all by itself. When serving, use grated aged pecorino toscano *cheese, a staple of Tuscan cooking, if you can find it. It has a sharper flavor than* parmigiano *and complements the rich taste of the soup.*

1	CUP DRIED BORLOTTI, PINTO, OR CRANBERRY BEANS
1	CUP ITALIAN SMALL BROWN LENTILS OR FRENCH GREEN LENTILS
½	CUP DRIED GREEN SPLIT PEAS
3	OUNCES PANCETTA (SEE INGREDIENT GUIDE ON PAGE 19)
1	SMALL RED ONION

1	MEDIUM CARROT
1	RIB CELERY
1	LARGE CLOVE GARLIC, PEELED
15	STEMS FRESH ITALIAN FLAT-LEAF PARSLEY, LEAVES ONLY
2	TABLESPOONS OLIVE OIL
2	BAY LEAVES
	SALT AND FRESHLY GROUND BLACK PEPPER
6	OUNCES DRIED SMALL TUBULAR PASTA SUCH AS TUBETTI OR DITALINI
	GRATED AGED PECORINO TOSCANO CHEESE OR PARMIGIANO CHEESE, FOR SERVING

Soak the borlotti beans in cold water for 8 hours or longer. Soak the lentils and peas in cold water for 4 hours. Drain all the beans and discard the soaking water. Rinse under cold water and drain again.

Finely chop together on a cutting board (or use a food processor) the pancetta, onion, carrot, celery, garlic, and parsley.

Heat the olive oil in a heavy 6-quart soup pot or casserole over medium heat. Add the chopped pancetta and vegetable mixture and cook slowly, about 5 minutes, until the pancetta begins to render its fat and the onion is soft.

Add the beans, bay leaves, and 12 cups cold water and place over medium-high heat. When the water begins to boil, lower the heat and simmer, about 2 hours, until the beans are tender. Remove and discard the bay leaves, season with salt and pepper to taste, and add the pasta. Raise the heat and continue cooking, stirring frequently to prevent the pasta from sticking to the bottom of the pot, 10 to 12 minutes longer, until the pasta is tender but firm to the bite, al dente. Serve with grated pecorino toscano cheese.

MAKES 6 SERVINGS

Zuppa di fagioli, pasta, e pomodoro

SOUP OF BORLOTTI, PASTA, AND TOMATO

Borlotti *are the "meatiest" of all the beans, which makes this simple but wonderfully flavorful soup a satisfying main course. You can prepare the beans ahead and add the pasta just before you want to serve it.*

1	CUP DRIED BORLOTTI, PINTO, OR CRANBERRY BEANS
2	CLOVES GARLIC, PEELED AND FINELY CHOPPED
1	MEDIUM CARROT, FINELY CHOPPED
1	RIB CELERY, FINELY CHOPPED
¼	CUP OLIVE OIL, PLUS MORE FOR SERVING
1½	CUPS CANNED WHOLE PEELED TOMATOES, COARSELY CHOPPED, WITH THEIR JUICE
6	LARGE LEAVES FRESH BASIL, CHOPPED
8	STEMS FRESH ITALIAN FLAT-LEAF PARSLEY, LEAVES ONLY, CHOPPED
	PINCH OF PEPERONCINO (RED PEPPER FLAKES)
	SALT
4	OUNCES DRIED EGG FETTUCCINE, BROKEN INTO PIECES
	GRATED PARMIGIANO CHEESE, FOR SERVING

Soak the beans in cold water for 8 hours or longer. Drain and discard the soaking water. Rinse under cold water and drain again. Combine the beans with the garlic, carrot, celery, olive oil, tomatoes, basil, parsley, peperoncino, and 8 cups of cold water in a heavy 6-quart soup pot or casserole over medium-high heat. When the water begins to boil, lower the heat and simmer, about 1 hour, until the beans are tender. Season with salt to taste. Add the pasta and cook, stirring frequently to prevent the pasta from sticking to the bottom of the pot, 10 to 12 minutes, until the pasta is tender but firm to the bite, al dente. Serve with parmigiano cheese.

MAKES 4 SERVINGS

ROTINI PASTA WITH WHITE BEAN SAUCE

The creamy cannellini goes exquisitely well with a squiggly-shaped pasta; the beans cling to the ridges and edges. I tasted this dish at a restaurant in Florence, Enoteca Pasta e Vino in the via San Niccolo.

½   CUP DRIED CANNELLINI OR GREAT NORTHERN BEANS

1   STEM FRESH ROSEMARY

3   LARGE CLOVES GARLIC, PEELED, 1 WHOLE, 2 FINELY CHOPPED

⅓   CUP OLIVE OIL

    PINCH OF PEPERONCINO (RED PEPPER FLAKES)

    SALT

12   OUNCES DRIED SQUIGGLY PASTA, SUCH AS ROTINI, FUSILLI, OR CAVATAPPI

8   STEMS FRESH ITALIAN FLAT-LEAF PARSLEY, LEAVES ONLY, CHOPPED

Soak the beans in cold water for 8 hours or longer. Drain and discard the soaking water. Rinse under cold water and drain again. Combine the beans, rosemary, the whole clove of garlic, and 6 cups cold water in a heavy medium saucepan over medium-high heat. When the water begins to boil, lower the heat and simmer, uncovered, about 1 hour, until the beans are tender. Drain and reserve ½ cup of the cooking liquid.

Combine the beans and the reserved cooking liquid in a food processor or blender, or use an immersion hand blender, and process until they are mashed, not pureed. They shouldn't be perfectly smooth.

Heat the olive oil in a large saucepan over medium-low heat. Add the chopped garlic and peperoncino and cook, stirring, about 2 minutes, being careful not to brown the garlic. Add the mashed beans, season with salt to taste, and continue cooking and stirring, about 5 minutes longer.

Meanwhile, bring a large pot of water to a boil over high heat. Add 1 tablespoon salt and the pasta and cook, stirring, about 8 minutes, until the pasta is almost tender. You want it to be slightly undercooked, because you will continue cooking it in the bean sauce. Reserve ½ cup of the pasta water and drain the pasta.

Transfer the pasta to the pan with the beans. Add the reserved pasta water. Turn the heat to medium and continue cooking, stirring frequently to prevent the pasta from sticking to the bottom of the pot, about 5 minutes, until the sauce has a creamy consistency and the pasta is tender but firm to the bite, al dente.

Garnish each serving with parsley.

MAKES 4 SERVINGS

Tagliatelle a ragù lucchese

PASTA WITH RED BEAN SAUCE

In Italy, fagioli rossi, *red kidney beans, are grown almost exclusively in the area around Lucca in Tuscany. This simple but very flavorful sauce can be served on any strand pasta.*

½	CUP DRIED RED KIDNEY BEANS
2	BAY LEAVES
1	LARGE CLOVE GARLIC, PEELED
	SALT
2	OUNCES PANCETTA (SEE INGREDIENT GUIDE ON PAGE 19)
1	MEDIUM RED ONION
1	RIB CELERY
½	CUP OLIVE OIL
	FRESHLY GROUND BLACK PEPPER
12	OUNCES DRIED TAGLIATELLE, LINGUINE, OR FETTUCCINE, BROKEN INTO THIRDS
8	STEMS FRESH ITALIAN FLAT-LEAF PARSLEY, LEAVES ONLY, CHOPPED
	FRESHLY GRATED PARMIGIANO CHEESE

Soak the beans in cold water for 8 hours or longer. Drain and discard the soaking water. Rinse under cold water and drain again. Combine the beans with the bay leaves and garlic in a medium saucepan with 6 cups cold water over medium-high heat. When the water begins to boil, lower the heat and simmer, about 1½ hours, until the beans are very tender. You want them to be falling apart. Remove and discard the bay leaves and garlic clove. Season with salt to taste, turn off the heat, and set aside.

Chop the pancetta, onion, and celery together, preferably in a food processor, or on a cutting board. Heat the olive oil in a heavy large saucepan over medium-low heat.

Add the pancetta mixture and cook, stirring, about 20 minutes, until the pieces of pancetta are brown and the onion is soft. Drain the beans and add them to the pancetta mixture. Cook, stirring, about 5 minutes. Season with salt and pepper to taste.

Meanwhile, bring a large pot of water to a boil over high heat. Add 1 tablespoon salt and the pasta and cook, stirring occasionally, 10 to 12 minutes, until the pasta is tender but firm to the bite, al dente. Drain the pasta and add it to the skillet with the beans. Stir in the parsley and toss well to combine. Serve with parmigiano cheese.

Makes 4 servings

CALABRIA-STYLE PASTA WITH BEANS

This is a robust, rustic recipe from the toe of Italy's boot. The name millecosedde *means "one thousand little things" and comes from the variety of beans that are simmered together to the consistency of a thick sauce. Pecorino romano or pecorino sardo cheese, both hard, grating cheeses made from sheep's milk, will add a savory, sharp accent to this rich pasta dish.*

¼	CUP ITALIAN SMALL BROWN LENTILS OR ANY BROWN LENTILS
⅓	CUP CHICKPEAS
¼	CUP CICERCHIE OR CHICKPEAS
⅓	CUP DRIED CANNELLINI OR GREAT NORTHERN BEANS
⅓	CUP DRIED SPLIT, SKINNED FAVA BEANS
1	OUNCE DRIED PORCINI MUSHROOMS (SEE INGREDIENT GUIDE ON PAGE 19)
4	CUPS FINELY SHREDDED SAVOY CABBAGE
1	MEDIUM YELLOW ONION, CHOPPED
1	RIB CELERY, FINELY CHOPPED
½	CUP OLIVE OIL
	SALT AND FRESHLY GROUND BLACK PEPPER
1	POUND DRIED SPAGHETTI, BROKEN INTO THIRDS
	GRATED PECORINO ROMANO OR PECORINO SARDO CHEESE, FOR SERVING

Soak all the beans together in cold water for 8 hours or longer. Drain and discard the soaking water. Rinse under cold water and drain again.

Soak the mushrooms in 2 cups warm water for 30 minutes. Drain, rinse under cold water, and chop.

Combine the beans with the mushrooms, cabbage, onion, and celery in a heavy 6-quart soup pot or casserole. Add 12 cups cold water, stir to combine, and place over medium-high heat. When the water begins to boil, lower the heat and simmer, uncovered, about $1\frac{1}{2}$ hours, until all the beans are tender. Stir in the oil and season with salt and pepper to taste. Add the pasta and continue cooking, stirring frequently to prevent the pasta from sticking to the bottom of the pot, 10 to 12 minutes, until the pasta is tender but firm to the bite, al dente. Cover and let stand about 5 minutes before serving so the flavors have a chance to combine. Serve with grated cheese.

MAKES 6 SERVINGS

PENNE WITH CHICKPEAS, SPLIT PEAS, AND BORLOTTI

This pasta dish from northern Italy is prepared with a mix of beans and seasoned with rosemary. You can substitute one bean for another or add additional varieties, but try to keep the overall quantity of beans the same.

¼ CUP ITALIAN SMALL BROWN LENTILS OR FRENCH GREEN LENTILS

½ CUP CHICKPEAS

¼ CUP DRIED GREEN SPLIT PEAS

½ CUP DRIED BORLOTTI, PINTO, OR CRANBERRY BEANS

1 LARGE RED ONION, CHOPPED

1 LEEK, WHITE PART ONLY, ROOT END REMOVED, RINSED BETWEEN THE LAYERS AND CHOPPED

2 CLOVES GARLIC, PEELED AND CHOPPED

5 STEMS FRESH ITALIAN FLAT-LEAF PARSLEY, LEAVES ONLY, CHOPPED

1 HEAPING TABLESPOON CHOPPED FRESH ROSEMARY LEAVES

¼ CUP OLIVE OIL

SALT AND FRESHLY GROUND BLACK PEPPER

8 OUNCES DRY PENNE PASTA

GRATED PARMIGIANO CHEESE, FOR SERVING

Soak the beans in cold water for 8 hours or longer. Drain and discard the soaking water. Rinse under cold water and drain again. Combine the beans with the onion, leek, garlic, parsley, rosemary, olive oil, and 8 cups cold water in a heavy 6-quart soup pot or casserole over medium-high heat. When the water begins to boil, lower the heat and simmer, uncovered, 1½ to 2 hours, until the beans are tender and the consistency of a thick sauce. Season with salt and pepper to taste.

Bring a large pot of water to a boil over high heat. Add 1 tablespoon salt and the pasta and cook, stirring occasionally, 10 to 12 minutes, until tender but firm to the bite, al dente. Drain the pasta, reserving the cooking water. Add the pasta to the beans with about 1 cup of the pasta-cooking water (depending on how thick or soupy the bean sauce is) and cook 2 to 3 minutes longer to combine the pasta with the sauce. Serve with parmigiano cheese.

MAKES 4 SERVINGS

PASTA WITH CICERCHIE AND MUSHROOMS

In Puglia, where this recipe comes from, fresh cardoncelli *mushrooms, so-named because they grow on the roots of the cardoon plant in the early spring, are used to prepare this dish. I found that the fresh oyster mushrooms in our markets come close to the flavor and the firm texture of the* cardoncelli. *If they are not available, you can use any other kind of fresh mushrooms. I tasted this pasta dish at a restaurant in Altamura.* Cicerchie, *a variety of chickpea, are grown in that area.*

1	CUP CICERCHIE OR CHICKPEAS
1	BAY LEAF
	SALT
1	POUND DRIED ORECCHIETTE PASTA
½	CUP OLIVE OIL, PLUS MORE FOR SERVING
1	POUND FRESH OYSTER MUSHROOMS, STEMMED, CAPS CUT INTO 1-INCH PIECES
	FRESHLY GROUND BLACK PEPPER
2	CLOVES GARLIC, PEELED

Soak the beans in cold water for 8 hours or longer. Drain and discard the soaking water. Rinse under cold water and drain again. Combine the beans and bay leaf in a heavy medium saucepan with 6 cups cold water over medium-high heat. When the water begins to boil, lower the heat and simmer, uncovered, about 1 hour, or until the beans are tender. Remove and discard the bay leaf, turn off the heat, and set aside.

Bring a large pot of water to a boil over high heat. Add 1 tablespoon salt and the pasta and cook, stirring occasionally, 10 to 12 minutes, until the pasta is tender but firm to the bite, al dente. Drain.

Meanwhile, heat ¼ cup olive oil in a large heavy skillet over medium heat. Add the mushrooms, season with salt and pepper to taste, and cook, stirring frequently, 7 to 10 minutes, or until tender. Turn off the heat and set aside. Reheat just before serving.

Drain the beans and reserve 1 cup of the cooking water. Heat the remaining ¼ cup olive oil in a heavy 6-quart soup pot or casserole over medium-low heat. Add the garlic and cook about 5 minutes, just until it begins to brown, being careful not to burn it. Remove the garlic from the pot and add the beans. Cook, stirring, 2 to 3 minutes. Add the pasta and the reserved cooking water from the beans. Season with salt to taste. Continue cooking about 5 minutes longer, until the pasta and beans are hot and the liquid has thickened.

Serve in soup bowls. Top each serving with some of the mushrooms. Season with pepper and a drizzle of olive oil.
Makes 6 servings

PASTA WITH SPINACH AND CHICKPEAS

One of my favorite recipes, this pasta and bean dish from the Tuscan coast is simple but very flavorful. You want to use a pasta shape that complements the chickpeas, like orecchiette, *little round disks, or a loosely twisted shape like* cavatappi.

1	CUP CHICKPEAS
2	LARGE CLOVES GARLIC, PEELED, 1 WHOLE, 1 FINELY CHOPPED
3	LARGE LEAVES FRESH SAGE
3	TABLESPOONS OLIVE OIL, PLUS MORE FOR SERVING
4	OUNCES PANCETTA (SEE INGREDIENT GUIDE ON PAGE 19), JULIENNED
4	OUNCES FRESH SPINACH LEAVES, STEMMED, RINSED, AND COARSELY CHOPPED (ABOUT 4 CUPS CHOPPED)
	SALT
10	OUNCES DRIED ORECCHIETTE PASTA
	FRESHLY GROUND BLACK PEPPER
	GRATED PARMIGIANO CHEESE, FOR SERVING

Soak the chickpeas in cold water for 8 hours or longer. Drain and discard the soaking water. Rinse under cold water and drain again. Combine the chickpeas with the whole clove of garlic, sage, and 6 cups cold water in a heavy medium saucepan over medium-high heat. When the water begins to boil, lower the heat and simmer, uncovered, about 1½ hours, until the chickpeas are tender. Remove and discard the garlic and sage. Drain the chickpeas and reserve 1 cup of the cooking liquid. Set aside.

Heat the olive oil in a heavy 6-quart soup pot or casserole. Add the chopped garlic and the pancetta and cook over low heat, about 10 minutes, until the pancetta begins to brown. Stir in the spinach and saute 2 to 3 minutes, until it is wilted. Add the chickpeas and the reserved liquid and continue cooking, stirring occasionally, 15 minutes.

Meanwhile, bring a large pot of water to a boil over high heat. Add 1 tablespoon of salt and the pasta and cook, stirring occasionally, 10 to 12 minutes, until the pasta is tender but firm to the bite, al dente. Drain the pasta and add to the chickpeas and spinach. Season with salt and pepper to taste and cook about 1 minute longer. Add a drizzle of olive oil to each serving. Serve with parmigiano cheese.

MAKES 4 SERVINGS

CALABRIAN FAVA BEANS AND PASTA

Macco is a thick puree of fava beans and pasta that's served throughout Italy on the 19th of March, the festival of San Giuseppe. In different parts of Italy, it may be prepared with different beans. This recipe with favas, tomatoes, and spaghetti is typical of Calabria, the southernmost region in Italy. It's always seasoned with lots of black pepper and served with a drizzle of olive oil and grated pecorino romano or pecorino sardo.

1 CUP DRIED SPLIT, SKINNED FAVA BEANS

1 MEDIUM RED ONION, CHOPPED

2 CLOVES GARLIC, FINELY CHOPPED

½ CUP CANNED CHOPPED TOMATOES, WITH THEIR JUICE

SALT

8 OUNCES DRIED SPAGHETTI, BROKEN INTO THIRDS

1 TEASPOON FINELY GROUND BLACK PEPPER

¼ CUP OLIVE OIL, PLUS MORE FOR SERVING

GRATED PECORINO ROMANO OR PECORINO SARDO CHEESE, FOR SERVING

Soak the beans in cold water for 8 hours or longer. Drain and discard the soaking water. Rinse under cold water and drain again. Combine the beans with the onion, garlic, tomatoes, and 6 cups cold water in a heavy 8-quart soup pot or casserole over medium-high heat. When the water begins to boil, lower the heat and simmer, uncovered, about 1 hour, until the beans are the consistency of a thick sauce. Season with salt to taste, turn off the heat, and set aside.

Meanwhile, bring a large pot of water to a boil over high heat. Add 1 tablespoon of salt and the pasta and cook, stirring occasionally, 10 to 12 minutes, until the pasta is tender but firm to the bite, al dente. Drain the pasta and add to the pot with the bean sauce. Stir in the pepper and olive oil.

Add a drizzle of olive oil and some grated cheese to each serving.

MAKES 4 SERVINGS

Lagane e fagioli

PASTA WITH CANNELLINI BEANS

This is a traditional recipe from Basilicata in southern Italy. Lagane are lasagna noodles, prepared only with flour, water, and salt—no eggs. Use dried lasagna pasta, made without egg, but break the sheets into smaller pieces before cooking; otherwise, they'll be unwieldy to eat.

1 CUP DRIED CANNELLINI OR GREAT NORTHERN BEANS

2 BAY LEAVES

SALT

¼ CUP OLIVE OIL, PLUS MORE FOR SERVING

1 LARGE CLOVE GARLIC, PEELED AND FINELY CHOPPED

4 OUNCES PANCETTA (SEE INGREDIENT GUIDE ON PAGE 19), FINELY CHOPPED

PINCH OF PEPERONCINO (RED PEPPER FLAKES)

8 OUNCES DRIED LASAGNA PASTA, PREPARED WITHOUT EGG, BROKEN INTO 2-INCH PIECES

FRESHLY GROUND BLACK PEPPER

GRATED PARMIGIANO CHEESE, FOR SERVING

Soak the beans in cold water for 8 hours or longer. Drain and discard the soaking water. Rinse under cold water and drain again. Combine the beans with the bay leaves and 6 cups cold water in a medium saucepan over medium-high heat. When the water begins to boil, lower the heat and simmer, uncovered, about 1 hour, until the beans are tender. Season with salt, remove and discard the bay leaves, turn off the heat, and set aside.

Heat the olive oil in a heavy large skillet over low heat. Add the garlic and pancetta and cook, stirring frequently, about 10 minutes, until the pancetta begins to brown. Stir in the peperoncino. Drain the beans, reserving 1 cup of the cooking water, and add them to the pancetta. Turn off the heat.

Meanwhile, bring a large pot of water to a boil over high heat. Add 1 tablespoon salt and the pasta and cook, stirring occasionally, 10 to 12 minutes, until the pasta is tender but firm to the bite, al dente. Drain the pasta and add to the beans along with the reserved cooking water. Lower the heat to medium-high and cook, stirring, about 5 minutes, until the sauce is thick. Season with salt and pepper to taste and mix well to combine.

Add a drizzle of olive oil and some parmigiano cheese to each serving.

MAKES 4 SERVINGS

Pasta e fagioli all'ischitana

PASTA AND CANNELLINI ISCHIA-STYLE

This simple but rich and flavorful dish from the island of Ischia, off the Mediterranean coast of Italy, near Naples, is traditionally made with a combination of three or four different types of pasta, a mix called mischiata. Often it's thick and thinner variations of spaghetti, including spaghettini and bucatini. This is traditionally a way to use up the odds and ends of pasta shapes that accumulate over the course of a week. You can also use just one type of pasta, with equally delicious results.

1	CUP DRIED CANNELLINI OR GREAT NORTHERN BEANS
¼	CUP OLIVE OIL
1	CUP CANNED CHOPPED TOMATOES, WITH THEIR JUICE
1	CLOVE GARLIC, PEELED AND FINELY CHOPPED
5	LARGE LEAVES FRESH BASIL, CHOPPED
1	RIB CELERY, FINELY CHOPPED
	SALT
4	OUNCES PANCETTA (SEE INGREDIENT GUIDE ON PAGE 19), CUT INTO SMALL DICE
	PINCH OF PEPERONCINO (RED PEPPER FLAKES)
8	OUNCES DRIED SPAGHETTI OR A COMBINATION OF SPAGHETTI, LINGUINE, SPAGHETTINI, AND BUCATINI, BROKEN INTO THIRDS
	GRATED PARMIGIANO CHEESE, FOR SERVING

Soak the beans in cold water for 8 hours or longer. Drain and discard the soaking water. Rinse under cold water and drain again. Combine the beans in a heavy 6-quart soup pot or casserole with the oil, tomatoes with their juice, garlic, basil, celery, and 8 cups cold water over medium-high heat. When the water begins to boil, lower the heat and simmer, uncovered, about 1 hour, until the beans are tender. Season with salt to taste, turn off the heat, and set aside.

Place the pancetta in a small saucepan over medium-low heat. Cook, stirring frequently, about 15 minutes, until the pancetta is brown and crisp. Add the pancetta and peperoncino to the beans and cook an additional 5 minutes.

Meanwhile, bring a large pot of water to a boil over high heat. Add 1 tablespoon salt and the pasta and cook, stirring occasionally, 5 minutes. The pasta will be very underdone. Drain and add the pasta to the beans and pancetta and continue cooking, 5 to 7 minutes longer, until the pasta is tender but firm to the bite, al dente, and the liquid has mostly been absorbed by the pasta. The bean and pasta mixture should be very thick. Serve with parmigiano cheese.

MAKES 4 SERVINGS

LIGURIAN PASTA AND CANNELLINI

Beans in Liguria come from the towns of Conio, Pigna, and Badalucco in the hills above the Mediterranean coast. This flavorful recipe from bean growers there is prepared with aromatic fresh herbs, garlic, and peperoncino (red pepper flakes). The original recipe calls for handmade pasta without egg, cut into small squares, quadrucci. I use lasagna *pasta, broken into smaller pieces before cooking.*

1	CUP FAGIOLI DI CONIO, CANNELLINI, OR GREAT NORTHERN BEANS
¼	CUP OLIVE OIL
1	LARGE RED ONION, CHOPPED
	PINCH OF PEPERONCINO (RED PEPPER FLAKES)

4	CUPS CHICKEN OR VEGETABLE BROTH
2	MEDIUM YUKON GOLD OR YELLOW FINN POTATOES, PEELED AND DICED
	SALT
8	OUNCES QUADRUCCI (1-INCH SQUARES) PASTA OR WIDE LASAGNA, BROKEN INTO SMALLER PIECES
1	LARGE CLOVE GARLIC, PEELED AND FINELY CHOPPED
8	STEMS FRESH ITALIAN FLAT-LEAF PARSLEY, LEAVES ONLY, CHOPPED
1	STEM FRESH ROSEMARY, LEAVES ONLY, CHOPPED
2–3	STEMS FRESH MARJORAM, LEAVES ONLY, CHOPPED
½	CUP FRESHLY GRATED PARMIGIANO CHEESE
	FRESHLY GROUND BLACK PEPPER

Soak the beans in cold water for 8 hours or longer. Drain and discard the soaking water. Rinse under cold water and drain again.

Heat the olive oil in a heavy 6-quart soup pot or casserole over medium-high heat. Add the onion and the peperoncino and cook, stirring, 2 to 3 minutes, until the onion begins to soften. Add the beans and broth. When the broth comes to a boil, lower the heat and simmer 45 minutes. Add the potatoes and continue cooking about 15 minutes longer, until the potatoes and the beans are tender. Turn off the heat and set aside.

Bring a large pot of water to a boil over high heat. Add 1 tablespoon of salt and the pasta and cook, stirring occasionally, 10 to 12 minutes, until the pasta is tender but firm to the bite, al dente. Drain the pasta and add to the pot with the beans. Stir in the garlic, parsley, rosemary, marjoram, and parmigiano cheese. Season with salt and pepper to taste. Cover the pot and allow to stand 15 to 20 minutes. Stir and serve.

MAKES 4 SERVINGS

TAGLIATELLE WITH LENTILS

In Bari, a large port city on the Adriatic Sea in Puglia, this sumptuous dish is traditionally prepared with fresh pasta that's made without eggs. Dried eggless pasta works just as well. Tria is the name for tagliatelle in the Pugliese dialect.

1½ CUPS ITALIAN SMALL BROWN LENTILS OR FRENCH GREEN LENTILS

1 CLOVE GARLIC, PEELED

2 BAY LEAVES

SALT

1 POUND DRIED TAGLIATELLE PASTA, BROKEN INTO THIRDS

½ CUP OLIVE OIL, PLUS MORE FOR SERVING

FRESHLY GROUND BLACK PEPPER

Combine lentils, garlic, bay leaves, and 6 cups cold water in a heavy medium saucepan over medium-high heat. When the water begins to boil, lower the heat and simmer gently, uncovered, 30 to 45 minutes, until the lentils are tender. Add salt to taste, remove the bay leaves, and set the lentils aside.

Meanwhile, bring a large pot of water to a boil. Add 1 tablespoon salt and the pasta and cook, stirring occasionally, 10 to 12 minutes, until al dente. Drain.

Heat the olive oil in a large pot over medium heat. Drain the lentils, reserving 1 cup of the cooking liquid. Add the lentils to the oil and stir well. Add pasta and reserved cooking liquid. Cook, stirring, 3 to 5 minutes, until the pasta and lentils are heated through and the sauce is thick. Season with pepper, and add a drizzle of olive oil to each serving.

MAKES 6 SERVINGS

Pasta e fagioli con la salsiccia

PASTA AND CANNELLINI WITH SAUSAGE

Prepare this marvelously flavorful dish with any sweet (not spicy) Italian sausage. You can also use ground pork. Cook the beans and sausage ahead of time, but add the pasta and finish cooking just before you plan to serve.

1   CUP DRIED CANNELLINI OR GREAT NORTHERN BEANS

3   LARGE LEAVES FRESH SAGE

1   CLOVE GARLIC, PEELED

½   POUND SWEET ITALIAN SAUSAGE (SEE INGREDIENT GUIDE ON PAGE 19), CASINGS REMOVED, OR GROUND PORK

1   CUP DRIED DITALINI OR TUBETTI PASTA
    SALT AND FRESHLY GROUND BLACK PEPPER

15 STEMS FRESH ITALIAN FLAT-LEAF PARSLEY, LEAVES ONLY, CHOPPED

Soak the beans in cold water for 8 hours or longer. Drain and discard the soaking water. Rinse under cold water and drain again. Combine the beans with the sage, garlic, and 10 cups cold water in a medium saucepan over medium-high heat. When the water begins to boil, lower the heat and simmer, uncovered, about 1 hour, until the beans are tender. Crumble the sausage or pork into the beans and cook, stirring, about 10 minutes, until the meat is no longer pink. Add the pasta and continue cooking, stirring frequently to prevent the pasta from sticking to the bottom of the pot, 10 to 12 minutes longer, until the pasta is tender but firm to the bite, al dente. Season with salt and pepper to taste. Stir in the parsley and serve.

MAKES 4 SERVINGS

Cavatellini con fagioli e cozze

PASTA WITH CANNELLINI
AND MUSSELS

This dish is served widely in Puglia, along the eastern Adriatic coast. The cavatellini *pasta has a shape and size that are a lot like the cannellini bean, except for the bean's indentation along one side. The* cavatellini *is essential to this dish, so it's worth hunting down.*

1	CUP DRIED CANNELLINI OR GREAT NORTHERN BEANS
3	CLOVES GARLIC, PEELED, 1 WHOLE, 2 CHOPPED
2	BAY LEAVES
½	CUP OLIVE OIL
3	FRESH PLUM TOMATOES, CORED, SEEDED, AND CHOPPED
2	POUNDS FRESH MUSSELS IN THEIR SHELLS, RINSED AND CLEANED OF ANY DIRT OR SAND; DISCARD ANY WITH BROKEN SHELLS
	SALT
8	OUNCES DRIED CAVATELLINI PASTA (SEE INGREDIENT GUIDE ON PAGE 19)
8	STEMS FRESH ITALIAN FLAT-LEAF PARSLEY, LEAVES ONLY, CHOPPED
15	LEAVES FRESH BASIL, CHOPPED
	FRESHLY GROUND BLACK PEPPER

Soak the beans in cold water for 8 hours or longer. Drain and discard the soaking water. Rinse under cold water and drain again. Combine the beans with the whole clove of garlic, the bay leaves, and 6 cups cold water over medium-high heat. When the water begins to boil, lower the heat and simmer, uncovered, stirring occasionally, about 1 hour, until the beans are tender. Drain. Remove and discard the garlic and bay leaves.

Heat the oil in a heavy 6-quart soup pot or casserole over medium heat. Add the chopped garlic and tomatoes and cook, 3 to 5 minutes, until the tomatoes begin to lose their fresh red color. Add the mussels, cover the pot, and simmer, about 10 minutes, until the shells open. Uncover and allow to cool. Remove the mussels from the shells, discarding any that haven't opened, and combine the mussels with the tomato sauce. Add the beans and simmer, about 10 minutes longer.

Meanwhile, bring a large pot of water to a boil over high heat. Add 1 tablespoon salt and the pasta and cook, stirring occasionally, 10 to 12 minutes, until the pasta is tender but firm to the bite, al dente. Drain the pasta and add to the mussels and beans. Stir in the parsley and basil and simmer about 5 minutes longer. Season with salt and pepper to taste.

MAKES 4 SERVINGS

PASTA SHELLS WITH CANNELLINI AND FILLET OF SOLE

In Italy, you'll find many dishes prepared with fish. This delicate sauce calls for fresh sole. The cherry tomatoes add intense flavor and color. This dish is not served with cheese.

½ CUP DRIED CANNELLINI OR GREAT NORTHERN BEANS

1 SMALL CARROT, FINELY CHOPPED

1 RIB CELERY, FINELY CHOPPED

½ MEDIUM RED ONION, FINELY CHOPPED

4 CLOVES GARLIC, PEELED, 2 WHOLE, 2 FINELY CHOPPED

3 BAY LEAVES

½ CUP OLIVE OIL

2 CUPS CHERRY TOMATOES, HALVED

PINCH OF PEPERONCINO (RED PEPPER FLAKES)

½ POUND FRESH SOLE FILLETS, CUT INTO 2-INCH PIECES

SALT

½ CUP DRY WHITE WINE

12 OUNCES DRIED CONCHIGLIETTE (SMALL SHELLS) PASTA

8 STEMS FRESH ITALIAN FLAT-LEAF PARSLEY, LEAVES ONLY, CHOPPED

Soak the beans in cold water for 8 hours or longer. Drain and discard the soaking water. Rinse under cold water and drain again. Combine the beans with the carrot, celery, onion, whole cloves of garlic, bay leaves, and 6 cups cold water in a medium saucepan over medium-high heat. When the water begins to boil, lower the heat and simmer, uncovered, stirring occasionally, about 1 hour, until the beans are tender. Drain. Remove and discard the garlic and bay leaves.

Heat the olive oil in a large skillet over medium heat. Add the chopped garlic, cherry tomatoes, and peperoncino and cook, about 3 minutes. Add the sole, season with salt to taste, and continue cooking while stirring, about 3 minutes longer. Add the wine and simmer about 10 minutes until it is mostly evaporated. Stir in the beans and continue cooking another 10 minutes.

Meanwhile, bring a large pot of water to a boil over high heat. Add 1 tablespoon salt and the pasta and cook, stirring occasionally, 10 to 12 minutes, until the pasta is tender but firm to the bite, al dente. Drain and add the pasta to the fish and bean sauce. Stir in the parsley and cook 2 to 3 minutes longer.

MAKES 4 SERVINGS

Fagioli are essential to a variety of main-course dishes. Those prepared with rice, polenta, *farro,* and barley traditionally have their place as *primi,* first courses, in the Italian meal hierarchy. But in Italy today, meals often become streamlined, and it's not uncommon to find first courses such as risotto and polenta served as *secondi,* main courses. These are satisfying, filling dishes that can easily be the centerpiece of a meal.

I recommend using Italian-grown rice—arborio or one of the other rice varieties such as *carnaroli* or *vialone nano*—and Italian-grown *farro,* a particular variety of whole wheat. These grains will ensure that you get the most authentic flavor from your cooking. I also recommend Italian-grown barley and Italian polenta, which is made from cornmeal. But if these are not available, you can prepare satisfying dishes with American-grown grains. When choosing a cornmeal for polenta, I find that the stone-ground variety has the best flavor.

The bean cuisine of Italy encompasses a wide assortment of main-course dishes prepared with meat: mostly straightforward stews and casseroles. These recipes require long, slow simmering until the beans are tender and flavorful and the meat is falling-apart tender.

When choosing cuts of meat that are best for this type of cooking, remember that the fattier cuts, such as the shoulder, leg, and breast, tend to be better suited to slow, moist cooking than the leaner loins and ribs. Similarly, fowl with dark meat—squab, duck, and chicken thighs—make the best partners for braised bean dishes.

The combination of seafood and beans is another option for main courses. When simmering fish and beans together, it is best to use fish that is well-suited to slow, moist cooking. This can include cod, sole, and monkfish. Grilled tuna or swordfish is also delicious when paired with beans served on the side. Most any and all shellfish are perfect for bean preparations.

Keep in mind, the main course of an Italian meal often follows one or two courses. Servings are meant to be modest but satisfying.

Minestra di riso e lenticchie

STEW OF RICE AND LENTILS

Umbrian lentils are considered the best, and most expensive, in Italy. They are grown in the small hilltown of Castelluccio. This classic Umbrian stew of rice and lentils is savory, and it can be prepared quickly and easily with only a few ingredients.

½	CUP ITALIAN SMALL BROWN LENTILS OR FRENCH GREEN LENTILS
3	TABLESPOONS OLIVE OIL
15	STEMS FRESH ITALIAN FLAT-LEAF PARSLEY, LEAVES ONLY, CHOPPED
1	CLOVE GARLIC, PEELED AND FINELY CHOPPED
1	CUP ARBORIO OR OTHER ITALIAN RICE (SEE INGREDIENT GUIDE ON PAGE 19)
2	TABLESPOONS TOMATO PASTE
2	CUPS HOT CHICKEN BROTH
	SALT AND FRESHLY GROUND BLACK PEPPER

Combine the lentils with 6 cups cold water in a medium saucepan over medium-high heat. When the water begins to boil, lower the heat and simmer, uncovered, about 45 minutes, until the lentils are tender.

Meanwhile, heat the olive oil in a heavy medium saucepan with a lid over medium heat. Add the parsley and garlic and cook, stirring, about 1 minute. Add the rice and stir well to combine with the parsley and garlic. Stir the tomato paste into the broth and add to the rice. When it begins to simmer, lower the heat, cover the pan, and simmer, about 20 minutes, until the rice is tender but firm to the bite, al dente. Season with salt and pepper to taste.

As soon as the rice is finished cooking, strain the lentils and add to the rice. Stir well to combine and serve.

MAKES 4 SERVINGS

FRIULI-STYLE RICE
AND FAGIOLI DI LAMON

The town of Pravisdomini, where this rice dish is a specialty, is just to the northwest of Venice. It's not a risotto, but it is creamy and very rich tasting. The beans of choice there are fagioli di Lamon, *but you can use* borlotti, pinto, *or cranberry beans. Serve with a lot of freshly grated* parmigiano *or* grana *(see Ingredient Guide on page 19) cheese.*

1   CUP DRIED FAGIOLI DI LAMON, BORLOTTI, PINTO, OR CRANBERRY BEANS

3   OUNCES PANCETTA (SEE INGREDIENT GUIDE ON PAGE 19)

1   MEDIUM RED ONION

1   RIB CELERY

2   TABLESPOONS OLIVE OIL

2   BAY LEAVES

2   MEDIUM YUKON GOLD OR YELLOW FINN POTATOES, PEELED AND DICED

6   CUPS CHICKEN BROTH

¾   CUP ARBORIO OR OTHER ITALIAN RICE (SEE INGREDIENT GUIDE ON PAGE 19)

SALT AND FRESHLY GROUND BLACK PEPPER

GRATED PARMIGIANO CHEESE, FOR SERVING

Soak the beans in cold water for 8 hours or longer. Drain and discard the soaking water. Rinse under cold water and drain again.

Finely chop the pancetta, onion, and celery together, preferably in a food processor, or on a cutting board.

Heat the olive oil in a heavy 6-quart casserole over medium heat. Add the pancetta mixture and cook, stirring, about 3 minutes, until the vegetables begin to soften. Add the beans, bay leaves, potatoes, and broth. Raise the heat to medium-high. When the broth begins to boil, lower the heat and simmer, uncovered, about 1 hour, until the beans are tender. Discard the bay leaves and set aside.

Twenty minutes before you plan to serve, bring the beans back to a boil and add the rice. Cook, stirring almost constantly to prevent the rice from sticking to the bottom of the pot, until the rice is tender but still firm to the bite, about 20 minutes. Season with salt and pepper to taste. Ladle into bowls and serve with parmigiano cheese.

MAKES 4 SERVINGS

Riso alla valtellina

BRAISED RICE, CANNELLINI, AND KALE

This is a traditional dish from Lombardy, where many varieties of rice are grown. Lombardy is mostly a flat plain with the Po River running through it, which makes it ideal for rice cultivation. You can use any variety of kale in this recipe. If you can find the Tuscan, it most resembles the Italian cavolonero.

1	CUP DRIED CANNELLINI OR GREAT NORTHERN BEANS
4	LARGE LEAVES FRESH SAGE
1	BUNCH GREEN KALE, PREFERABLY DINOSAUR OR TUSCAN, STEMMED AND COARSELY CHOPPED
1	CUP ARBORIO OR OTHER ITALIAN RICE (SEE INGREDIENT GUIDE ON PAGE 19)
	SALT AND FRESHLY GROUND BLACK PEPPER
2	TABLESPOONS UNSALTED BUTTER
	GRATED PARMIGIANO CHEESE, FOR SERVING

Soak the beans in cold water for 8 hours or longer. Drain and discard the soaking water. Rinse under cold water and drain again. Combine the beans with the sage and 6 cups cold water in a medium saucepan over medium-high heat. When the water begins to boil, lower the heat and simmer, uncovered, about 1 hour, until the beans are tender. Turn off the heat and set aside.

Meanwhile, bring a large pot of water to a boil over high heat. Add the kale and cook 5 minutes. Drain, allow to cool, and press as much water from it as you can. Turn it onto a cutting board and chop.

Combine the kale and rice in a heavy 6-quart casserole with 4 cups cold water over medium-high heat. When the water begins to boil, lower the heat, cover the pot, and simmer, stirring occasionally, about 20 minutes, until the rice is tender but firm to the bite, al dente.

Drain the beans and add them to the rice. Season with salt and pepper to taste. Stir in the butter and continue cooking, 2 to 3 minutes longer. Serve with parmigiano cheese.

MAKES 6 SERVINGS

RISOTTO WITH BLACK-EYED PEAS AND CRISP PANCETTA

This recipe comes from the Ristorante al Pino in Lombardy. Black-eyed peas are becoming more common in Italian restaurants, but they are still considered a "new" ingredient in most Italian homes. You can use small white beans if black-eyed peas are not available.

½   CUP BLACK-EYED PEAS OR GREAT NORTHERN BEANS

3   TABLESPOONS UNSALTED BUTTER

2   TABLESPOONS OLIVE OIL

1   YELLOW ONION, FINELY CHOPPED

1   CUP ARBORIO OR OTHER ITALIAN RICE (SEE INGREDIENT GUIDE ON PAGE 19)

½   CUP DRY WHITE WINE

3   CUPS HOT CHICKEN OR MEAT BROTH

⅓   CUP GRATED PARMIGIANO CHEESE, PLUS MORE FOR SERVING

5   STEMS FRESH ITALIAN FLAT-LEAF PARSLEY, LEAVES ONLY, CHOPPED

4   OUNCES PANCETTA (SEE INGREDIENT GUIDE ON PAGE 19), CUT INTO SMALL DICE

Soak the beans in cold water for 8 hours or longer. Drain and discard the soaking water. Rinse under cold water and drain again. Combine the beans with 6 cups cold water in a medium saucepan over medium-high heat. When the water begins to boil, lower the heat and simmer, uncovered, 45 minutes to 1 hour, until the beans are tender. Drain the beans and reserve the cooking liquid.

Heat 2 tablespoons butter and 1 tablespoon olive oil in a heavy 6-quart casserole over medium-low heat. When the butter is melted, add the onion and cook, stirring, 2 to 3 minutes, until the onion begins to soften. Raise the heat to medium-high, add the rice, and cook, while stirring, about 2 minutes, to thoroughly coat the grains with the butter and oil mixture. Stir in the wine and continue cooking until the wine is mostly evaporated.

Meanwhile, heat the broth to simmering in a separate small saucepan over medium heat. Begin to add the broth to the rice, ½ cup at a time, stirring frequently, until each addition has mostly evaporated.

After 10 minutes, add the beans and ½ cup of their cooking liquid and stir until it has mostly evaporated. Con-tinue to add the broth, ½ cup at a time, until the rice is tender but firm to the bite, al dente, about 10 minutes longer. Stir in the last addition of broth, the remaining 1 ta-blespoon butter, parmigiano cheese, and parsley. Continue to stir until the butter is melted and the cheese is incorpo-rated into the risotto.

While the risotto is cooking, combine the pancetta and the remaining 1 tablespoon olive oil in a small saucepan over medium-low heat. Cook, stirring, 10 to 15 minutes, until the pancetta is crisp and brown. Turn off the heat and use a slotted spoon to transfer the pancetta to a paper towel to drain.

To serve, spoon the risotto into preheated bowls and top each serving with a tablespoon of the crisp pancetta. Serve with more parmigiano cheese at the table.

MAKES 4 SERVINGS

PAVIA-STYLE RISOTTO WITH BORLOTTI

Pavia sits in one of Italy's most fertile agricultural areas. It is known for several gastronomic pleasures, including white peaches and zuppa parese, *a traditional soup that is essentially consommé and poached egg. Pavia is also known for its risotto. This simple but very rich risotto is prepared with red wine that gives the rice a lovely claret color.*

½ CUP DRIED BORLOTTI, PINTO, OR CRANBERRY BEANS

8 LEAVES FRESH SAGE, PLUS MORE TO GARNISH SERVING DISHES

3 TABLESPOONS OLIVE OIL

2 OUNCES PANCETTA (SEE INGREDIENT GUIDE ON PAGE 19), CUT INTO SMALL DICE

1 CUP ARBORIO OR OTHER ITALIAN RICE (SEE INGREDIENT GUIDE ON PAGE 19)

½ CUP DRY RED WINE

8 CUPS CHICKEN OR MEAT BROTH

2 TABLESPOONS UNSALTED BUTTER

⅓ CUP GRATED PARMIGIANO CHEESE, PLUS MORE FOR SERVING

SALT AND FRESHLY GROUND BLACK PEPPER

Soak the beans in cold water for 8 hours or longer. Drain and discard the soaking water. Rinse under cold water and drain again. Combine the beans with 4 sage leaves, 2 tablespoons olive oil, and 6 cups cold water in a medium saucepan over medium-high heat. When the water begins to boil, lower the heat and simmer, uncovered, about 1 hour, until the beans are tender. Drain and discard the sage.

Heat the remaining 1 tablespoon olive oil in a heavy 6-quart casserole over medium-low heat. Add the pancetta and cook, stirring occasionally, until it begins to brown, about 10 minutes. Raise the heat to medium-high, add the rice, and cook, while stirring, about 2 minutes, to thoroughly coat the grains with the pancetta and oil mixture.

Stir in the beans and wine and continue cooking until the wine is mostly evaporated.

Meanwhile, heat the broth to simmering in a separate small saucepan over medium heat. Begin to add the broth to the rice, ½ cup at a time, stirring frequently, until each addition has mostly evaporated. Continue to add the broth, ½ cup at a time, until the rice is tender but firm to the bite, al dente, about 20 minutes. Add the last addition of broth, butter, and parmigiano cheese. Stir until the butter is melted and the cheese is incorporated into the risotto. Season with salt and pepper to taste. Serve in preheated bowls. Garnish each serving with some fresh sage leaves and serve with more parmigiano cheese on the side.

MAKES 4 SERVINGS

PEASANT-STYLE RISOTTO WITH BORLOTTI AND CABBAGE

A contadina is a farmer or field worker. This simple, rustic recipe, made with cabbage and beans, comes from the Po River valley of Lombardy, where most of the rice for risotto grows. Although the ingredients are modest, this risotto is deliciously creamy and rich.

½ CUP DRIED BORLOTTI, PINTO, OR CRANBERRY BEANS

6 LARGE LEAVES FRESH SAGE, 3 WHOLE, 3 CHOPPED

3 CUPS FINELY SHREDDED GREEN CABBAGE

2 TABLESPOONS OLIVE OIL

2 OUNCES PANCETTA (SEE INGREDIENT GUIDE ON PAGE 19), CUT INTO SMALL DICE

1 CUP ARBORIO OR OTHER ITALIAN RICE (SEE INGREDIENT GUIDE ON PAGE 19)

½ CUP DRY WHITE WINE

2 TABLESPOONS TOMATO PUREE

3 CUPS CHICKEN BROTH

2 TABLESPOONS UNSALTED BUTTER

½ CUP GRATED PARMIGIANO CHEESE, PLUS MORE FOR SERVING

5 STEMS FRESH ITALIAN FLAT-LEAF PARSLEY, LEAVES ONLY, CHOPPED

SALT AND FRESHLY GROUND BLACK PEPPER

Soak the beans in cold water for 8 hours or longer. Drain and discard the soaking water. Rinse under cold water and drain again. Combine the beans with 3 whole sage leaves and 6 cups cold water in a medium saucepan over medium-high heat. When the water begins to boil, lower the heat and simmer, uncovered, about 1 hour, until the beans are tender. Drain and discard the sage.

Meanwhile, bring a medium saucepan of water to a boil over high heat. Add the cabbage and boil for 5 minutes. Drain and set aside.

Heat the olive oil in a heavy 6-quart casserole over medium-low heat. Add the pancetta and cook, stirring occasionally, until it begins to brown, about 10 minutes. Raise the heat to medium-high, add the rice, and cook, while stirring, about 2 minutes, to thoroughly coat the grains with the pancetta and oil mixture. Stir in the wine and continue cooking until the wine is mostly evaporated. Add the tomato puree, cabbage, and beans.

Meanwhile, heat the broth to simmering in a separate small saucepan over medium heat. Begin to add the broth to the rice, ½ cup at a time, stirring frequently, until each addition is mostly incorporated into the rice. Continue to add the broth, ½ cup at a time, until the rice is tender but firm to the bite, al dente, about 20 minutes. Add the last addition of broth, the butter, parmigiano cheese, parsley, and chopped sage. Stir until the butter is melted and the cheese is incorporated into the risotto. Season with salt and pepper to taste. Serve in preheated bowls with more parmigiano cheese on the side.

MAKES 4 SERVINGS

VENETO-STYLE RISOTTO WITH BORLOTTI

In this enticing risotto, the beans are cooked with vegetables and pureed, then added to the risotto at the very end of cooking, making the finished dish surprisingly rich and creamy.

½ CUP DRIED BORLOTTI, PINTO, OR CRANBERRY BEANS

2 RIBS CELERY, CHOPPED

1 MEDIUM RED ONION, COARSELY CHOPPED

1 MEDIUM CARROT, CHOPPED

1 LARGE CLOVE GARLIC, PEELED

2 OUNCES PROSCIUTTO (SEE INGREDIENT GUIDE ON PAGE 19), CHOPPED

3 LARGE LEAVES FRESH SAGE

SALT

3 TABLESPOONS UNSALTED BUTTER

2 TABLESPOONS OLIVE OIL

½ YELLOW ONION, FINELY CHOPPED

1 CUP ARBORIO OR OTHER ITALIAN RICE (SEE INGREDIENT GUIDE ON PAGE 19)

½ CUP DRY WHITE WINE

5 CUPS CHICKEN BROTH

½ CUP GRATED PARMIGIANO CHEESE, PLUS MORE FOR SERVING

FRESHLY GROUND BLACK PEPPER

Soak the beans in cold water for 8 hours or longer. Drain and discard the soaking water. Rinse under cold water and drain again. Combine the beans with the celery, red onion, carrot, garlic, prosciutto, sage, and 6 cups cold water in a medium saucepan over medium-high heat. When the water begins to boil, lower the heat and simmer, uncovered, about 1 hour, until the beans are tender. Season with salt to taste. Drain the beans and vegetables, transfer them to a food processor or blender, and process until smooth. Set aside.

Heat 1 tablespoon butter and the olive oil in a heavy 6-quart casserole over medium-low heat. When the butter is melted, add the yellow onion and cook, stirring, 2 to 3 minutes, until the onion begins to soften. Raise the heat to medium-high, add the rice, and cook, while stirring, about 2 minutes, to thoroughly coat the grains with the butter and oil mixture. Stir in the wine and continue cooking until the wine is mostly evaporated.

Meanwhile, heat the broth to simmering in a separate small saucepan over medium heat. Begin to add the broth to the rice, ½ cup at a time, stirring frequently, until each addition has mostly evaporated. Continue to add the broth, ½ cup at a time, until the rice is tender but firm to the bite, al dente, about 20 minutes. Add the last addition of broth, bean and vegetable puree, remaining 2 tablespoons butter, and parmigiano cheese. Stir until the butter is melted and the cheese is incorporated into the risotto. Season with salt and pepper to taste. Serve in preheated bowls with more parmigiano cheese on the side.

MAKES 4 SERVINGS

POLENTA WITH FAGIOLI DI LAMON AND TOMATO SAUCE

The chef at the Antica Trattoria Boschetti near Udine in Friuli prepared this dish for me in the late summer when the fagioli di Lamon were fresh from their pods. It's a savory combination of beans with onions and prosciutto di San Daniele—which comes from the town of San Daniele, only a few miles away—and a straightforward tomato sauce served over soft, creamy polenta. This is definitely a restaurant dish with three separate preparations, but it's worthy of the extra effort. You can prepare the beans and the tomato sauce ahead of time.

BEANS

1	CUP DRIED FAGIOLI DI LAMON, BORLOTTI, PINTO, OR CRANBERRY BEANS
1	TABLESPOON OLIVE OIL
1	SMALL RED ONION, FINELY CHOPPED
2	OUNCES PROSCIUTTO DI SAN DANIELE (SEE INGREDIENT GUIDE ON PAGE 19), THINLY SLICED AND CUT INTO 1-INCH PIECES
5	STEMS FRESH ITALIAN FLAT-LEAF PARSLEY, LEAVES ONLY, CHOPPED
	SALT AND FRESHLY GROUND BLACK PEPPER

TOMATO SAUCE

1/4	CUP OLIVE OIL
1	SMALL RED ONION, FINELY CHOPPED
1	MEDIUM CARROT, FINELY CHOPPED
1	CLOVE GARLIC, PEELED AND FINELY CHOPPED
2	LARGE LEAVES FRESH BASIL, CHOPPED
2	CUPS CANNED CHOPPED TOMATOES, WITH THEIR JUICE
	SALT AND FRESHLY GROUND BLACK PEPPER

POLENTA

1 CUP YELLOW POLENTA (SEE INGREDIENT GUIDE ON PAGE 19)

½ TABLESPOON SALT

To prepare the beans: Soak the beans in cold water for 8 hours. Drain and discard the water. Rinse under cold water and drain again. Combine the beans with 6 cups cold water in a saucepan, bring to a boil, lower the heat, and simmer, uncovered, about 1 hour, until the beans are tender. Drain and set aside.

Heat the oil in a saucepan over medium heat. Add the onion, prosciutto, and parsley and cook, stirring, about 10 minutes, until the onion is translucent. Add the beans, season with salt and pepper, and cook about 1 minute longer. Set aside. Reheat before serving.

To prepare the tomato sauce: Heat the oil in a medium saucepan over medium heat. Add the onion, carrot, garlic, and basil and cook, stirring, 2 to 3 minutes, until the onion begins to soften. Add the tomatoes and season with salt and pepper. When the sauce simmers, cover the pan and cook slowly, stirring occasionally, about 1 hour. Transfer the sauce to a blender or food processor. Process until smooth. Return the sauce to the pan and reheat before serving.

To prepare the polenta: Combine the polenta and salt in a heavy medium saucepan. Gradually add 2 cups cold water while stirring briskly with a wire whisk. Place the pan over medium-low heat and stir continuously, about 5 minutes, until the polenta begins to thicken. Continue cooking, stirring frequently, about 40 minutes longer. The polenta should be thick and leave the sides of the pot. Turn off the heat and allow the polenta to stand for 2 to 3 minutes before serving.

To serve, spoon some polenta onto plates. Top with beans and tomato sauce.

MAKES 4 SERVINGS

Polenta incantata

LIGURIAN POLENTA WITH BORLOTTI AND VEGETABLES

Incantata *means enchanted, and this polenta is a marvelous, hearty winter dish from southern Liguria. The recipe was originally created as an economical and substantial alternative to meat when times were difficult. Still popular today, this version comes from a restaurant called Ristorante Il Castello da Marco in Castelnuovo Magra. I recommend chopping all the vegetables, except the potatoes, in the food processor. The fine texture gives the finished dish a pleasing consistency. Leftover cold* polenta incantata *becomes* polenta croccante *when you cut it into squares and pan-fry it in vegetable oil until it's deliciously crisp and crunchy. Drain it well on paper towels before serving.*

1   CUP DRIED BORLOTTI, PINTO, OR CRANBERRY BEANS

1   SMALL BUNCH GREEN KALE, STEMMED, RINSED, AND FINELY CHOPPED

1   MEDIUM CARROT, FINELY CHOPPED

1   MEDIUM RED ONION, FINELY CHOPPED

1   CLOVE GARLIC, PEELED AND FINELY CHOPPED

3   MEDIUM YUKON GOLD OR YELLOW FINN POTATOES, PEELED AND CHOPPED

¼   CUP OLIVE OIL, PLUS MORE FOR SERVING

1   CUP YELLOW POLENTA (SEE INGREDIENT GUIDE ON PAGE 19)

SALT AND FRESHLY GROUND BLACK PEPPER

GRATED PARMIGIANO CHEESE, FOR SERVING

Soak the beans in cold water for 8 hours or longer. Drain and discard the soaking water. Rinse under cold water and drain again. Combine the beans with the kale, carrot, onion, garlic, potatoes, olive oil, and 8 cups cold water in a heavy 6-quart casserole over medium-high heat. When the water begins to boil, lower the heat and simmer, uncovered, 30 minutes. The beans will not be fully cooked. Add the polenta, a little bit at a time, stirring well to incorporate each addition into the vegetables. (If you add too much at once, it may become lumpy.) Continue cooking, stirring frequently, about 45 minutes longer. Season with salt and pepper to taste. The polenta should be thick, not stiff. If it becomes stiff, add a little hot water and continue to stir. Serve in deep, hot dishes with a drizzle of olive oil and a generous serving of parmigiano cheese.

MAKES 6 SERVINGS

POLENTA, BORLOTTI, AND PANCETTA FROM THE VENETO

Polenta e fagioli al veneto

In the Veneto, borlotti *beans and* fagioli di Lamon *are traditionally served with polenta, as in this superb main course of tomato and bean sauce spooned over polenta and garnished with crispy pancetta.*

1½ CUPS BORLOTTI, FAGIOLI DI LAMON, PINTO, OR CRANBERRY BEANS

¼ CUP OLIVE OIL

2 MEDIUM RED ONIONS, FINELY CHOPPED

2 CLOVES GARLIC, PEELED AND FINELY CHOPPED

2 CUPS CANNED CHOPPED TOMATOES, WITH THEIR JUICE

1 TABLESPOON RED WINE VINEGAR

2 TABLESPOONS TOMATO PASTE

1 CUP CHICKEN OR VEGETABLE BROTH

10 LEAVES FRESH BASIL, FINELY CHOPPED

4 LEAVES FRESH SAGE, FINELY CHOPPED

SALT AND FRESHLY GROUND BLACK PEPPER

2 CUPS YELLOW POLENTA (SEE INGREDIENT GUIDE ON PAGE 19)

6 OUNCES PANCETTA (SEE INGREDIENT GUIDE ON PAGE 19), CUT INTO ¼-INCH DICE

Soak the beans in cold water for 8 hours or longer. Drain and discard the water. Rinse under cold water and drain again. Combine the beans with 6 cups cold water in a saucepan over medium-high heat. When the water begins to boil, lower the heat and simmer, uncovered, about 1 hour, until the beans are tender. Turn off the heat and set aside.

Heat the olive oil in a heavy 6-quart casserole over medium heat. Add the onions and garlic and cook, stirring, about 3 minutes, until the onions begin to soften. Stir in the chopped tomatoes and the vinegar. Dissolve the tomato paste in the broth and add to the onion and tomatoes with the basil and sage. Season with salt and pepper to taste and simmer, 15 to 20 minutes, until the sauce is thick.

Drain the beans and add to the tomato sauce. Stir well to combine. Continue cooking 15 minutes longer. (You can prepare this ahead of time. Reheat before serving.)

Combine the cornmeal with 1 tablespoon salt in a heavy 6-quart pot over medium heat. Gradually whisk in 9 cups cold water and place over medium heat, stirring constantly, until the polenta begins to boil. Lower the heat and simmer, stirring frequently with a wooden spoon, for 45 minutes, until thick.

Meanwhile, place the pancetta in a small saucepan over low heat. Cook, stirring frequently, until the meat turns brown and crisp, about 15 minutes. Use a slotted spoon to transfer the pancetta to a paper towel to drain.

To serve, spoon the polenta into preheated serving dishes. Ladle the beans over the polenta and top with the crispy pancetta.

MAKES 6 SERVINGS

CANNELLINI AND FARRO WITH SUMMER VEGETABLES

Farro is an ancient variety of whole wheat that is still grown in Tuscany and Umbria. Its texture is a lot like that of barley. Prepare this salad in the summer when vegetables are most flavorful. Cook the vegetables separately until tender, being careful not to overcook them so they don't fall apart when tossing the salad. Serve the salad at room temperature or warm, but not hot.

½ CUP DRIED CANNELLINI OR GREAT NORTHERN BEANS

5 LEAVES FRESH SAGE

3 LARGE CLOVES GARLIC, PEELED

1 CUP FARRO (SEE INGREDIENT GUIDE ON PAGE 19)

SALT

¼ POUND GREEN BEANS, ENDS TRIMMED

1–2 MEDIUM ZUCCHINI, ENDS TRIMMED, HALVED LENGTHWISE, AND CUT INTO ½-INCH SLICES

1 SMALL YUKON GOLD OR YELLOW FINN POTATO, PEELED AND CUT INTO 1-INCH PIECES

2 MEDIUM CARROTS, HALVED LENGTHWISE AND CUT INTO ½-INCH SLICES

4 OUNCES PANCETTA (SEE INGREDIENT GUIDE ON PAGE 19), CUT IN SMALL DICE

¼ CUP OLIVE OIL

PINCH OF PEPERONCINO (RED PEPPER FLAKES)

FRESHLY GROUND BLACK PEPPER

Soak the beans in cold water for 8 hours or longer. Drain and discard the soaking water. Rinse under cold water and drain again. Combine the beans with sage, 1 clove of garlic, and 6 cups cold water in a medium saucepan over medium-high heat. When the water begins to boil, lower the heat and simmer, uncovered, about 1 hour, until the beans are tender. Drain and discard the sage and garlic.

Meanwhile, soak the farro in cold water for 30 minutes. Drain and discard the soaking water. Combine the farro with 4 cups cold water in a medium saucepan over medium-high heat. When the water begins to boil, lower the heat and simmer, stirring occasionally, uncovered, about 45 minutes, until the farro is tender. Drain and rinse under cold water. Transfer to a large mixing bowl, cover with plastic wrap, and set aside.

Meanwhile, bring a large saucepan of water to a boil over medium-high heat. Add 1 tablespoon salt. Cook each of the vegetables separately in the boiling water. Remove with a strainer, rinse under cold water, and transfer to a large mixing bowl. Cook the green beans for 6 minutes; zucchini for 3 minutes; potatoes for 5 minutes; and carrots for 5 minutes.

In a small saucepan, combine the pancetta with the olive oil, peperoncino, and the remaining 2 cloves garlic and cook over low heat, 10 to 15 minutes, until the pancetta is brown and crisp. Remove and discard the garlic cloves.

Add the farro and cooked beans to the vegetables. Pour the pancetta and olive oil mixture over the farro and mix well to combine. Season with salt and pepper to taste.

MAKES 4 SERVINGS

BEANS AND GRAINS FROM CILENTO

This recipe comes from Baronessa Cecilia Baratta, a charming woman who raises water buffalo that produce milk for mozzarella cheese. The baronessa also runs a wonderful agriturismo (bed and breakfast) near Capaccio in southern Campania. It is a local tradition there to prepare this dish in the spring, both to finish off the dried beans and grains from winter storage and as an offering for a good growing season. The beans and grains are cooked separately, then eaten together, flavored only with salt and olive oil.

¼ CUP CHICKPEAS

¼ CUP DRIED CANNELLINI OR GREAT NORTHERN BEANS

¼ CUP ITALIAN SMALL BROWN LENTILS OR FRENCH GREEN LENTILS

¼ CUP DRIED SPLIT, SKINNED FAVA BEANS

¼ CUP CICERCHIE OR CHICKPEAS

SALT

½ CUP FARRO (SEE INGREDIENT GUIDE ON PAGE 19)

1½ CUPS PEARL BARLEY

OLIVE OIL FOR SERVING

Soak the beans together in cold water for 8 hours or longer. Drain and discard the soaking water. Rinse under cold water and drain again. Combine the beans with 8 cups cold water in a heavy 6-quart casserole over medium-high heat. When the water begins to boil, lower the heat and simmer, uncovered, 1 to 1½ hours, until the beans are tender. Season with salt and set aside.

Meanwhile, soak the farro and barley together in a small bowl with cold water to cover for 1 hour. Drain and discard the water and transfer the grains to a medium saucepan with fresh cold water to cover. Place over medium-high heat and bring the water to a boil. Add salt to taste, lower the heat, and simmer, uncovered, about 45 minutes, until the grains are tender but still slightly chewy. Drain.

Serve the grain mixture in individual soup bowls. Drain the beans and spoon them over the grains. Generously drizzle olive oil over each serving.

MAKES 4 SERVINGS

Spezzatino di salsiccia, fave, e fagioli

STEW OF SAUSAGES, FRESH FAVAS, AND CANNELLINI BEANS

This recipe comes from the Ristorante L'Ambasciata in Quistello in Lombardy. Chef Romano Tamani is one of Italy's best-known and highly rated chefs. He uses well-seasoned sausages made from cinghiale, *fresh wild boar, to prepare this dish. You can use any flavorful sausage you like. Fresh fava beans require both shelling from their large green pods and peeling the skin from each bean on all but the smallest, greenest ones. They're worth the extra work.

1	CUP DRIED CANNELLINI OR GREAT NORTHERN BEANS
1	STEM FRESH MARJORAM PLUS 1 TABLESPOON CHOPPED FRESH MARJORAM LEAVES
6	TABLESPOONS OLIVE OIL
6	FRESH SAUSAGES, PREFERABLY WILD BOAR SAUSAGE (SEE INGREDIENT GUIDE ON PAGE 19), CASINGS REMOVED, CUT INTO 2-INCH PIECES
2	CUPS CHICKEN BROTH
1	CUP PEELED FRESH FAVA BEANS (ABOUT 2 POUNDS IN THEIR PODS)
	SALT AND FRESHLY GROUND BLACK PEPPER

Soak the beans in cold water for 8 hours or longer. Drain and discard the water. Rinse under cold water and drain again. Combine the beans with the stem of marjoram and 6 cups cold water in a saucepan over medium-high heat. When the water begins to boil, lower the heat and simmer, uncovered, about 1 hour, until the beans are tender. Drain and set aside.

Heat the olive oil in a heavy 6-quart casserole over medium heat. Add the sausages and cook, about 5 minutes, until they are beginning to brown. Add the broth and beans, cover the casserole, and cook, about 30 minutes, until the sausages are cooked through and the broth has thickened. Add the fava beans and continue cooking, uncovered, 10 minutes longer. Stir in the chopped marjoram and season with salt and pepper to taste. Serve in deep soup plates.

MAKES 4 SERVINGS

Fagioli della sagra

STEW OF CANNELLINI, VEAL, AND SAUSAGES

This rich and flavorful stew, originally from Liguria, is delicious with some good crusty bread or with polenta or pasta. Finely chop the vegetables and garlic together in a food processor, if you have one, or on a cutting board.

2   CUPS FAGIOLI DI CONIO, CANNELLINI, OR GREAT NORTHERN BEANS

3   TABLESPOONS OLIVE OIL

1   MEDIUM RED ONION, FINELY CHOPPED

1   CARROT, FINELY CHOPPED

1   RIB CELERY, FINELY CHOPPED

1   LARGE CLOVE GARLIC, PEELED AND FINELY CHOPPED

8   STEMS FRESH ITALIAN FLAT-LEAF PARSLEY, LEAVES ONLY, FINELY CHOPPED

½   POUND VEAL STEW MEAT, CUT INTO 2-INCH PIECES

½   POUND SWEET ITALIAN SAUSAGE (SEE INGREDIENT GUIDE ON PAGE 19), CASINGS REMOVED, OR GROUND PORK

1   CUP DRY WHITE WINE

½   CUP TOMATO PUREE

1   TABLESPOON TOMATO PASTE

PINCH OF PEPERONCINO (RED PEPPER FLAKES)

3   CUPS CHICKEN BROTH

SALT

Soak the beans in cold water for 8 hours or longer. Drain and discard the soaking water. Rinse under cold water and drain again.

Heat the olive oil in a heavy 6-quart casserole over medium heat. Add the onion, carrot, celery, garlic, and parsley and cook, stirring, 2 to 3 minutes, until the vegetables begin to soften. Add the veal and sausage, crumbling the sausage into the pan, and continue cooking until it loses its raw color, about 5 minutes. Add the wine and let it evaporate slowly, about 10 minutes. Add the tomato puree, tomato paste, and peperoncino. Stir in the beans and broth. Cover the pot and simmer, 1 to 1½ hours, until the veal is tender enough to cut with a wooden spoon and the beans are tender. Season with salt to taste, and serve.

MAKES 6 SERVINGS

Lenticchie con salsicce

STEW OF LENTILS AND SAUSAGE

Sausage with lentils is a tantalizing combination. This simple stew of sausages and lentils in a rich tomato broth is from Umbria. It is a flavorful main course to serve with polenta (see Basic Polenta on page 28).

1 CUP ITALIAN SMALL BROWN LENTILS OR FRENCH GREEN LENTILS

2 RIBS CELERY, 1 CUT IN LARGE PIECES, 1 FINELY CHOPPED

2 CLOVES GARLIC, PEELED, 1 WHOLE, 1 FINELY CHOPPED

SALT

¼ CUP OLIVE OIL

2 POUNDS SWEET ITALIAN SAUSAGE (SEE INGREDIENT GUIDE ON PAGE 19), CASINGS REMOVED, CUT INTO 2-INCH PIECES, OR GROUND PORK

1 CUP TOMATO PUREE

2 CUPS CHICKEN OR MEAT BROTH

FRESHLY GROUND BLACK PEPPER

5 STEMS FRESH ITALIAN FLAT-LEAF PARSLEY, LEAVES ONLY, CHOPPED

Combine the lentils with the large pieces of celery and whole clove of garlic in a medium saucepan with 6 cups cold water over medium-high heat. When the water begins to boil, lower the heat and simmer, uncovered, about 30 minutes, until the lentils are barely tender. Season with salt to taste and drain.

Meanwhile, heat the olive oil in a heavy large skillet over medium heat. Add the chopped celery and chopped garlic and cook, stirring, 2 to 3 minutes, until the celery begins to soften. Add the sausage and cook, stirring, 3 to 5 minutes longer, until the meat loses its raw pink color. Add the lentils, tomato puree, and broth. Stir well to combine. When the liquid comes to a simmer, cover the skillet and cook slowly, about 30 minutes longer, until the sauce is thick. Season with salt and pepper to taste. Serve with polenta (see Basic Polenta on page 28). Garnish each serving with parsley.

MAKES 4 SERVINGS

STEW OF CHICKPEAS AND PORK

Although chickpeas are mostly associated with the cooking of southern Italy, this traditional northern Italian dish, served on All Souls' Day, comes from Milan. It is typically served with a vinegary condiment such as mostarda *(spicy pickled fruit) or* salsa verde, *a sharp-tasting green sauce like the one given here.*

STEW

- 1 CUP CHICKPEAS
- 2 LARGE STEMS FRESH ROSEMARY, 1 WHOLE, 1 LEAVES ONLY, FINELY CHOPPED
- SALT
- ¼ CUP OLIVE OIL
- 2–3 POUNDS BONELESS PORK SHOULDER, CUT INTO 3-INCH PIECES
- FRESHLY GROUND BLACK PEPPER
- ½ CUP DRY WHITE WINE
- 2 TABLESPOONS TOMATO PASTE
- 2 CUPS CHICKEN BROTH
- 2 MEDIUM RED ONIONS, CUT INTO LARGE PIECES
- 1 LARGE CARROT, CUT INTO 1-INCH PIECES
- 2 RIBS CELERY, CUT INTO 1-INCH PIECES

SALSA VERDE

- 3 TABLESPOONS CAPERS IN VINEGAR, DRAINED
- 1 ANCHOVY PACKED IN SALT, RINSED IN COLD WATER AND FILLETED, OR 2 ANCHOVY FILLETS PACKED IN OIL, DRAINED (SEE INGREDIENT GUIDE ON PAGE 19)
- 15 STEMS FRESH ITALIAN FLAT-LEAF PARSLEY, LEAVES ONLY
- 1 CLOVE GARLIC, PEELED
- ½ CUP EXTRA VIRGIN OLIVE OIL
- SALT AND FRESHLY GROUND BLACK PEPPER

To prepare the stew: Soak the chickpeas in cold water for 8 hours or longer. Drain and discard the soaking water. Rinse under cold water and drain again. Combine the beans, the whole stem of rosemary, and 6 cups cold water in a medium saucepan over medium-high heat. When the water begins to boil, lower the heat and simmer, about 1½ hours, until the beans are tender. Season with salt, discard the rosemary, turn off the heat, and set aside.

Meanwhile, heat the olive oil in a heavy 6-quart casserole over medium heat. Add the meat, season with salt and pepper, and lightly brown on all sides. Add the wine and cook slowly, about 10 minutes, until it has mostly evaporated. Dissolve the tomato paste in the broth and add to the meat with the onions, carrot, celery, and chopped rosemary. Bring the liquid to a boil, lower the heat, cover the pot, and simmer, stirring occasionally, about 2 hours.

To prepare the salsa verde: While the meat is cooking, combine the capers, anchovy, parsley, and garlic in a food processor or blender. Process until chopped, about 15 seconds. With the machine running, add the extra virgin olive oil in a steady stream. Scrape down the sides of the container and process about 30 seconds longer. Transfer the sauce to a small serving bowl, cover, and set aside.

When the meat is tender, drain the chickpeas and add them to the meat. Season with salt and pepper to taste. Simmer an additional 30 minutes. Serve with the salsa verde on the side.

MAKES 4 SERVINGS

Jota

TRIESTE-STYLE SOUP OF FAGIOLI DI LAMON, BACON, AND SAUERKRAUT

Rinaldo Krcivoj, owner, with his wife, Guia, of the Antica Trattoria Boschetti near Udine in Friuli, gave me this recipe. He explained that during the First World War, fought bitterly in and around the region, this substantial soup sustained the Italian troops. It's still popular there during the winter months. Smoked pancetta (see Ingredient Guide on page 19) or smoked bacon is essential to the soup's authentic flavor. This hearty soup is filling and satisfying enough to be an entree.

1 CUP DRIED FAGIOLI DI LAMON, BORLOTTI, PINTO, OR CRANBERRY BEANS

4 OUNCES SMOKED PANCETTA OR SMOKED SLAB BACON (SEE INGREDIENT GUIDE ON PAGE 19), CUT INTO DICE

1 CLOVE GARLIC, PEELED AND FINELY CHOPPED

1 SMALL YELLOW ONION, FINELY CHOPPED

5 STEMS FRESH ITALIAN FLAT-LEAF PARSLEY, LEAVES ONLY, CHOPPED

1 WHOLE BAY LEAF

3 LEAVES FRESH SAGE, CHOPPED

1 CUP SAUERKRAUT, RINSED UNDER COLD WATER AND DRAINED

1 MEDIUM YUKON GOLD OR YELLOW FINN POTATO, PEELED AND THINLY SLICED

SALT AND FRESHLY GROUND BLACK PEPPER

Soak the beans in cold water for 8 hours or longer. Drain and discard the soaking water. Rinse under cold water and drain again.

Combine the pancetta or bacon with the garlic and onion in a heavy 6-quart casserole over medium-low heat. Cook, stirring frequently, about 10 minutes, until the onion is soft and the meat begins to brown. Stir in the parsley, bay leaf, and sage and continue cooking, about 1 minute longer. Add the beans and 6 cups cold water. Raise the heat to medium-high. When the water begins to boil, lower the heat and simmer, uncovered, about 1 hour, until the beans are tender. Discard the bay leaf. Add the sauerkraut and potatoes and continue cooking, stirring occasionally, about 30 minutes longer, until the potatoes are tender and the soup has thickened slightly. Season with salt and pepper to taste, and serve.

MAKES 4 SERVINGS

Ola al forno

PIEMONTESE BRAISED VEAL WITH BORLOTTI AND VEGETABLES

This traditional peasant dish is from the mountains of Piemonte in northwestern Italy, where it was originally prepared in a ceramic pot, ola, and cooked slowly for hours in a wood-burning oven. You'll find that the beans and meat become incredibly tender and flavorful.

VEAL

1   CUP DRIED BORLOTTI, PINTO, OR CRANBERRY BEANS

4   TABLESPOONS OLIVE OIL

2   OUNCES PANCETTA, CUT INTO SMALL DICE

1   LARGE RED ONION, CHOPPED

1   RIB CELERY, CHOPPED

2   CLOVES GARLIC, PEELED AND CHOPPED

4–5   POUNDS VEAL OR PORK SHOULDER, BONED, TRIMMED, AND TIED

    SALT AND FRESHLY GROUND BLACK PEPPER

½   CUP DRY WHITE WINE

2   LEEKS, TRIMMED AND CLEANED, HALVED LENGTHWISE, AND CUT INTO ½-INCH SLICES

2   CARROTS, HALVED LENGTHWISE AND CUT INTO ½-INCH SLICES

10   LEAVES FRESH BASIL, CHOPPED

8   STEMS FRESH ITALIAN FLAT-LEAF PARSLEY, LEAVES ONLY, CHOPPED

4   CUPS CHICKEN OR MEAT BROTH

4   MEDIUM YUKON GOLD POTATOES, PEELED, HALVED LENGTHWISE, AND CUT INTO ½-INCH SLICES

SALSA VERDE

3	TABLESPOONS CAPERS IN VINEGAR, DRAINED
1	SALT-PACKED ANCHOVY, RINSED IN COLD WATER AND FILLETED, OR 2 OIL-PACKED ANCHOVY FILLETS
15	STEMS FRESH ITALIAN FLAT-LEAF PARSLEY, LEAVES ONLY
6	LARGE LEAVES FRESH BASIL
1	CLOVE GARLIC, PEELED
½	CUP EXTRA VIRGIN OLIVE OIL

To prepare the veal: Soak beans in cold water for 8 hours. Drain, discard water, rinse in cold water, and drain again.

Preheat the oven to 350 degrees.

Heat 2 tablespoons oil in a heavy 6-quart casserole over medium heat. Add pancetta, onion, celery, and garlic and cook, stirring, about 3 minutes, until onion softens. Set aside.

Heat remaining oil in a large skillet over medium heat. Add veal, season with salt and pepper, and brown on all sides, about 5 minutes. Add to the casserole with the pancetta mixture. Pour the wine into the skillet and cook,

scraping the sides and bottom of the pan, until reduced by half. Pour over the meat. Add the beans to the casserole, layering with the leeks and carrots around the meat. Sprinkle basil and parsley over the vegetables. Add the broth and bring to a simmer.

Cover the casserole and place it in the middle of the oven. Cook for 3 hours. Add the potatoes, cover, and cook 1 hour longer. Season with salt again, if necessary.

To prepare the salsa verde: Combine the capers, anchovies, parsley, basil, and garlic in a food processor. Process until chopped. With the machine running, add the extra virgin olive oil in a steady stream. Scrape down the sides of the container and process about 30 seconds longer. Transfer the sauce to a small serving bowl, cover, and set aside.

Slice the meat and serve in soup plates with beans, vegetables, and broth, with the sauce on the side.

MAKES 6 SERVINGS

Pennerelle con ceci

STEW OF BEEF SHIN AND CHICKPEAS

This simple but tasty stew of beef and chickpeas is the signature dish of the Ristorante San Pietrino in Rome, a restaurant owned by the DiMauro family. Paola DiMauro, matriarch of the family and the restaurant, discovered this old Roman recipe, which had disappeared for centuries. It has become a popular menu attraction, and is their piatto del ricordo—in Italy, memorable restaurant dishes are commemorated with souvenir plates.

1	CUP CHICKPEAS
2	CLOVES GARLIC, PEELED, 1 WHOLE, 1 FINELY CHOPPED
1	BAY LEAF
2	TABLESPOONS OLIVE OIL, PLUS MORE FOR SERVING
1	RIB CELERY, CHOPPED
3	POUNDS MEAT CUT FROM BEEF SHANK, SLICED INTO 2-INCH STRIPS
2	MEDIUM CARROTS, HALVED LENGTHWISE AND CUT INTO ½-INCH SLICES
½	POUND SMALL YELLOW CIPOLLINI, YELLOW BUTTON ONIONS, OR SMALL WHITE ONIONS, PEELED AND LEFT WHOLE
	SALT AND FRESHLY GROUND BLACK PEPPER

Soak the chickpeas in cold water for 8 hours or longer. Drain and discard the soaking water. Rinse under cold water and drain again. Combine the chickpeas with the whole clove of garlic, the bay leaf, and 6 cups cold water in a medium saucepan over medium-high heat. When the water begins to boil, lower the heat and simmer, uncovered, 1 hour, until the chickpeas are tender. Drain the chickpeas and reserve the cooking liquid. Discard the garlic and bay leaf.

Meanwhile, heat the olive oil in a heavy 6-quart casserole over medium heat. Add the chopped garlic and celery and cook, 1 to 2 minutes. Add the beef and saute, about 5 minutes, until the meat loses its raw, red color. Add the carrots, onions, chickpeas, and 3 cups of the reserved cooking liquid. Cover the casserole, lower the heat, and simmer, stirring occasionally, about 4 hours, until the meat is falling-apart tender. Season with salt. If the stew becomes dry during cooking, add small amounts of water as needed. Garnish each serving with black pepper and a drizzle of olive oil.

Makes 6 servings

LAMB STEW WITH WHITE BEANS FROM PIGNA

Pigna is a town in the Ligurian hills high above the Mediterranean Sea. The fagioli di Pigna, *a specialty there, are round white beans about the size of cannellini beans. This dish is traditionally made with* capra, *goat, but lamb is a good substitute. Be sure to cook the lamb slowly to ensure it becomes falling-off-the-bone tender.*

2	CUPS DRIED FAGIOLI DI PIGNA, CANNELLINI, OR GREAT NORTHERN BEANS
3	STEMS FRESH ROSEMARY
3	CLOVES GARLIC, PEELED, 1 WHOLE, 2 FINELY CHOPPED

	SALT
¼	CUP OLIVE OIL
1	MEDIUM RED ONION, FINELY CHOPPED
1	RIB CELERY, FINELY CHOPPED
1	CARROT, FINELY CHOPPED
	PINCH OF PEPERONCINO (RED PEPPER FLAKES)
2	BAY LEAVES
2–3	POUNDS BONELESS LAMB CUT FROM THE LEG, CUT INTO 3-INCH PIECES
1	CUP DRY WHITE WINE
3	CUPS CHICKEN OR MEAT BROTH

Soak the beans in cold water for 8 hours or longer. Drain and discard the soaking water. Rinse under cold water and drain again. Combine the beans with 1 stem of the rosemary, the whole clove of garlic, and 6 cups cold water in a large saucepan over medium-high heat. When the water begins to boil, lower the heat and simmer, uncovered, about 45 minutes, until the beans are tender. Turn off the heat, season with salt to taste, and set aside.

Meanwhile, heat the olive oil in a heavy 6-quart casserole over medium heat. Add the onion, celery, carrot, chopped garlic, peperoncino, the remaining 2 stems rosemary, and bay leaves and cook gently, 2 to 3 minutes, until the vegetables begin to soften. Add the lamb and season with salt. Cook, stirring, 5 to 7 minutes, until the meat is browned on all sides. Add the wine and simmer slowly, about 10 minutes, until it is mostly evaporated. Add the broth, lower the heat, and cover the pot. Simmer, stirring occasionally, 2 hours, until the meat is tender enough to cut with a wooden spoon.

Drain the beans, add them to the lamb, cover the pot, and cook 10 minutes longer. Remove and discard the rosemary stems before serving.

MAKES 6 SERVINGS

BRAISED LENTILS AND LAMB SHANKS

This is a robust dish that has full, hearty flavor. The original recipe is from Castelluccio in Umbria, where some of the best lentils in Italy are grown. I find the combination of lamb shanks and lentils irresistible.

4   TABLESPOONS OLIVE OIL

4   OUNCES PANCETTA (SEE INGREDIENT GUIDE ON PAGE 19), CHOPPED

3   CLOVES GARLIC, PEELED, 1 WHOLE, 2 FINELY CHOPPED

3   BAY LEAVES

½   CUP ITALIAN SMALL BROWN LENTILS OR FRENCH GREEN LENTILS

1   TABLESPOON RED WINE VINEGAR

4   LAMB SHANKS (ABOUT 3 POUNDS), CUT INTO 2-INCH PIECES (ASK THE BUTCHER TO CUT THEM FOR YOU)

     SALT AND FRESHLY GROUND BLACK PEPPER

1   STEM FRESH ROSEMARY

1   CUP DRY WHITE WINE

2   CUPS CHICKEN BROTH

Heat 2 tablespoons of the olive oil in a large saucepan over medium heat. Add half the pancetta, the whole garlic clove, and the bay leaves and cook, about 5 minutes, until the garlic begins to brown. Discard the garlic. Stir in the lentils and 4 cups cold water. Raise the heat to high. When the water begins to boil, lower the heat and simmer, uncovered, about 45 minutes to 1 hour, until the lentils are very tender. Discard the bay leaves, add the vinegar, and cook 1 minute longer. Turn off the heat and set aside.

Meanwhile, heat the remaining 2 tablespoons of olive oil in a heavy 6-quart casserole. Add the remaining pancetta and cook, stirring, about 5 minutes, until it begins to brown. Add the lamb, season with salt and pepper to taste, and cook, about 10 minutes, until the meat is brown on all sides. Add the chopped garlic, rosemary, and wine. Cook about 10 minutes, until the wine has mostly evaporated. Add the broth, cover, and simmer, about 1 hour, until the meat is tender. Discard the rosemary.

Drain the lentils and add them to the pot with the meat, stir well to combine, cover, and continue cooking, 30 minutes longer. Season with salt and pepper to taste and serve.

MAKES 6 SERVINGS

Anatra con lenticchie

BRAISED DUCK LEGS WITH LENTILS

This dish of duck legs and lentils is richly flavored and best served over creamy polenta (see Basic Polenta on page 28). Duck legs are available from better butchers and from online sources (see Ingredient Guide on page 19). The duck legs require skinning. You can do it easily with a sharp knife. For an added treat, cook the skin separately into delicious cracklings to serve on the side.

2   TABLESPOONS OLIVE OIL
2   CARROTS, FINELY CHOPPED
1   RIB CELERY, FINELY CHOPPED

1   MEDIUM RED ONION, FINELY CHOPPED
8   STEMS FRESH ITALIAN FLAT-LEAF PARSLEY, LEAVES ONLY, CHOPPED
6   FRESH DUCK LEGS WITH THIGHS, SKINNED
    SALT AND FRESHLY GROUND BLACK PEPPER
1   CUP DRY WHITE WINE
1   BAY LEAF
6   STEMS FRESH THYME
1   CUP ITALIAN SMALL BROWN LENTILS OR FRENCH GREEN LENTILS
4   CUPS CHICKEN BROTH

Heat the olive oil over medium heat in a heavy large skillet with a lid or a casserole big enough to hold the duck legs in a single layer. Add the carrots, celery, onion, and parsley and saute about 3 minutes, until the onion begins to soften. Move the vegetables to the side of the pan and add the duck legs. Season with salt and pepper and cook, about 7 minutes on each side, until lightly browned. Add the wine, bay leaf, and thyme and continue cooking, about 10 minutes longer, until the wine has mostly evaporated. Add the lentils and broth, bring to a simmer, cover the pan, and cook, 1 hour. Remove and discard the bay leaf and thyme stems. Season with salt and pepper to taste. Serve with polenta.

MAKES 6 SERVINGS

BRAISED PARTRIDGE WITH LENTILS

This savory stew comes from Sardinia, where partridge, or squab, is a traditional ingredient in the cuisine. Squab are available from better butchers and from online and mail-order sources (see Ingredient Guide on page 19), but you can also use Cornish hens.

2	TABLESPOONS OLIVE OIL
2	SQUAB OR CORNISH HENS, EACH CUT INTO 4 PIECES
	SALT AND FRESHLY GROUND BLACK PEPPER
2	OUNCES PANCETTA (SEE INGREDIENT GUIDE ON PAGE 19), CUT INTO SMALL DICE
1	MEDIUM RED ONION, FINELY CHOPPED
2	CLOVES GARLIC, PEELED AND FINELY CHOPPED
6	LARGE LEAVES FRESH SAGE, CHOPPED
½	CUP DRY RED WINE
1	CUP ITALIAN SMALL BROWN LENTILS OR FRENCH GREEN LENTILS
½	CUP TOMATO PUREE
2–3	CUPS CHICKEN BROTH

Heat the olive oil in a heavy 6-quart casserole over medium heat. Add the squab, season with salt and pepper to taste, and lightly brown, 3 to 5 minutes on each side. Remove the squab from the pan and add the pancetta. Cook, stirring, about 5 minutes, until the pancetta begins to render its fat. Add the onion, garlic, and sage and cook about 2 minutes longer, until the onion begins to soften.

Return the squab to the casserole and add the wine. Simmer, stirring occasionally, about 10 minutes, until the wine has mostly evaporated. Add the lentils, tomato puree, and enough broth to barely cover the meat and lentils. Stir to combine. When the liquid begins to boil, lower the heat, cover, and simmer, 45 minutes to 1 hour, until the sauce is thick, the lentils are tender, and the meat is cooked through. Add more salt and pepper to taste, if desired, and serve.

MAKES 6 SERVINGS

STEW OF CHICKEN WITH CANNELLINI

Livorno, on the Mediterranean coast of Tuscany, is best known for cacciuscco, a flavorful fish soup. But this delicious stew of chicken and white beans is also a flavorful local specialty. Serve with crusty bread and some fresh sauteed chard or kale. It goes well with a bottle of Tuscan wine such as Chianti or Rosso di Montalcino.

1	CUP DRIED CANNELLINI OR GREAT NORTHERN BEANS
2	CLOVES GARLIC, PEELED, 1 WHOLE, 1 FINELY CHOPPED
10	LARGE LEAVES FRESH SAGE, 4 WHOLE, 6 FINELY CHOPPED
3	TABLESPOONS OLIVE OIL
12	BONELESS, SKINLESS CHICKEN THIGHS
	SALT AND FRESHLY GROUND BLACK PEPPER
½	CUP DRY RED WINE
1 ½	CUPS HOT CHICKEN BROTH
2	TABLESPOONS TOMATO PASTE
8	STEMS FRESH ITALIAN FLAT-LEAF PARSLEY, LEAVES ONLY, CHOPPED

Soak the beans in cold water for 8 hours or longer. Drain and discard the soaking water. Rinse under cold water and drain again. Combine the beans with the whole clove of garlic, 4 sage leaves, and 6 cups cold water in a medium saucepan over high heat. When the water begins to boil, lower the heat and simmer, about 1 hour, until the beans are tender. Drain and set aside.

Meanwhile, heat the olive oil over medium-high heat in a heavy large skillet or casserole large enough to hold the chicken in a single layer. Add the chicken, season with salt and pepper, and cook, about 5 minutes on each side, until lightly browned. Stir in the remaining garlic and sage. Add the wine and cook, about 10 minutes, until it is mostly evaporated. Combine the broth and tomato paste and add to the meat. Cover the pan and simmer, about 20 minutes, until the meat is tender enough to cut with a wooden spoon.

Add the drained beans to the chicken and continue simmering, covered, about 10 minutes longer. Garnish each serving with parsley.

MAKES 6 SERVINGS

Petto di pollo con salvia e fagioli

BREAST OF CHICKEN WITH SAGE AND CANNELLINI

This is an elegant but simple dish from Puglia that calls for whole, boned chicken breasts with their skin. If you're not handy with a boning knife, have the butcher do it for you. The rolled breasts are seasoned with sage, sliced, and garnished with the beans in tomato sauce and zucchini to make a festive presentation in red, white, and green—the colors of the Italian flag.

2	CUPS DRIED CANNELLINI OR GREAT NORTHERN BEANS
12	LEAVES FRESH SAGE, 10 WHOLE, 2 FINELY CHOPPED
2	LARGE CLOVES GARLIC, PEELED, 1 WHOLE, 1 FINELY CHOPPED
	SALT
2	WHOLE CHICKEN BREASTS, BONED AND BUTTERFLIED, WITH SKIN ON
6	TABLESPOONS OLIVE OIL, PLUS MORE FOR SERVING
	FRESHLY GROUND BLACK PEPPER
2	OUNCES PANCETTA (SEE INGREDIENT GUIDE ON PAGE 19), THINLY SLICED
1	CUP TOMATO PUREE
1	MEDIUM ZUCCHINI, CUT INTO ¼-INCH ROUNDS

Soak the beans in cold water for 8 hours or longer. Drain and discard the soaking water. Rinse under cold water and drain again. Combine the beans, 2 whole sage leaves, the whole clove of garlic, and 6 cups cold water in a medium saucepan over medium-high heat. When the water begins to boil, lower the heat and simmer, about 1 hour, until the beans are tender. Add salt to taste, turn off the heat, and set aside. Discard the sage and garlic.

Preheat the oven to 425 degrees.

Place the chicken breasts, skin side down, on a cutting board. Season the meat with salt and place 4 sage leaves on each breast. Roll the meat into tight cylinders, so that the skin is on the outside. Tie in several places with kitchen string. Rub each breast with 1 tablespoon olive oil, season with salt and pepper, and wrap with the slices of pancetta. Place the rolled breasts on a baking sheet and place in the oven. Bake about 50 minutes, until the meat is lightly browned, the juices run clear when you test it with a sharp knife, and the pancetta is crisp. Remove from the oven and allow to rest for 2 to 3 minutes.

Meanwhile, heat the remaining 4 tablespoons olive oil in a medium saucepan over medium heat. Add the chopped garlic and chopped sage and cook, about 1 minute, being careful not to brown the garlic. Add the tomato puree and continue cooking, about 5 minutes. Drain the beans and add to the tomato sauce. Season with salt to taste and continue cooking, 10 to 15 minutes longer.

Place the zucchini in a steamer basket over boiling water and steam, 5 minutes. Season with salt to taste.

To serve, slice the chicken into 1- to 2-inch pieces. Spoon some of the beans onto each plate, pile some zucchini in the middle, and arrange some chicken slices in a semicircle around it. Drizzle olive oil over the chicken and serve.

MAKES 4 SERVINGS

STEW OF RABBIT WITH CHICKPEAS

Rabbit and hare are traditionally prepared in most areas of Italy. This combination of chickpeas and rabbit from Puglia is, to my taste, perfection. The creaminess of the beans complements the delicate flavor of the rabbit.

1½	CUPS CHICKPEAS
4	CLOVES GARLIC, PEELED, 1 WHOLE, 3 FINELY CHOPPED
2	BAY LEAVES
6	TABLESPOONS OLIVE OIL
1	RABBIT (3 POUNDS), CUT INTO 6 PIECES
	SALT AND FRESHLY GROUND BLACK PEPPER
1	STEM FRESH ROSEMARY, LEAVES ONLY, CHOPPED
1	CUP DRY WHITE WINE
2	CUPS CANNED CHOPPED TOMATOES, WITH THEIR JUICE
1	CUP CHICKEN BROTH

Soak the chickpeas in cold water for 8 hours or longer. Drain and discard the soaking water. Rinse under cold water and drain again. Combine the chickpeas with the whole clove of garlic, 1 bay leaf, 1 tablespoon olive oil, and 6 cups cold water in a heavy medium saucepan over medium-high heat. When the water begins to boil, lower the heat and simmer, uncovered, 1 to 1½ hours, until the chickpeas are tender. Drain and discard the bay leaf.

Meanwhile, heat the remaining 5 tablespoons olive oil in a heavy 6-quart casserole large enough to hold the rabbit in a single layer over medium heat. Add the rabbit pieces, season with salt and pepper, and brown on all sides. Sprinkle the chopped garlic and rosemary over the rabbit, add the wine, and simmer, about 10 minutes, until the wine is mostly evaporated. Stir in the chickpeas, tomatoes with their juice, and broth; season with salt and pepper to taste, cover the pot, and continue cooking, 45 minutes to 1 hour, until the rabbit is tender and the sauce is thick.

MAKES 4 SERVINGS

Guazzetto di pesce e fagioli cannellini

STEW OF CANNELLINI AND MONKFISH

Guazzetto usually refers to fish cooked in a light sauce, often with wine and tomato. It is a typical preparation in Lombardy, in northern Italy. This recipe comes from Cremona, an inland city where freshwater fish are plentiful. Where I live on the Atlantic coast, saltwater fish are more available, and I found that monkfish makes a delicious alternative. You can use any firm white-flesh fish you like, but cooking times will vary with different fish.

1 CUP DRIED CANNELLINI OR GREAT NORTHERN BEANS

6 LARGE LEAVES FRESH SAGE, 3 WHOLE, 3 FINELY CHOPPED

SALT

3 TABLESPOONS OLIVE OIL, PLUS MORE FOR SERVING

1 CLOVE GARLIC, PEELED AND FINELY CHOPPED

PINCH OF PEPERONCINO (RED PEPPER FLAKES)

2 PINTS CHERRY TOMATOES, HALVED

½ CUP DRY WHITE WINE

½ CUP FISH OR CHICKEN BROTH

8 STEMS FRESH ITALIAN FLAT-LEAF PARSLEY, LEAVES ONLY, CHOPPED

2 POUNDS MONKFISH TAILS, MEMBRANE REMOVED, OR OTHER WHITE FISH FILLETS, CUT INTO 2-INCH PIECES

Soak the beans in cold water for 8 hours or longer. Drain and discard the soaking water. Rinse under cold water and drain again. Combine the beans with 3 whole sage leaves and 6 cups cold water in a medium saucepan over medium-high heat. When the water begins to boil, lower the heat and simmer, uncovered, about 1 hour, until the beans are tender. Season with salt to taste. Turn off the heat and set aside. Discard the sage.

Heat the olive oil in a heavy 6-quart casserole over medium heat. Add the garlic, peperoncino, tomatoes, wine, and broth and simmer, about 10 minutes, until slightly reduced. Drain the beans and add them to the broth and tomatoes along with the parsley; continue cooking, about 5 minutes longer. Add the fish and season with salt to taste. Cover the pan and continue cooking, about 15 minutes longer, until the fish flakes easily with a fork. Add a drizzle of olive oil to each serving.

MAKES 4 SERVINGS

Zuppa di ceci e frutti di mare

SOUP OF CHICKPEAS AND SEAFOOD

Many versions of this recipe are found throughout Italy. This one, more stew than soup, is prepared with mussels, clams, and scallops. It comes from the Veneto.

1 CUP CHICKPEAS

1 MEDIUM YUKON GOLD OR YELLOW FINN POTATO, PEELED AND CUT INTO SMALL DICE

1 MEDIUM CARROT, FINELY CHOPPED

1 MEDIUM RED ONION, FINELY CHOPPED

1 RIB CELERY, FINELY CHOPPED

¼ CUP OLIVE OIL

1 CLOVE GARLIC, PEELED AND FINELY CHOPPED

1 POUND FRESH MUSSELS IN THEIR SHELLS, RINSED AND CLEANED OF ANY DIRT OR SAND; DISCARD ANY WITH BROKEN SHELLS

1 POUND FRESH LITTLENECK CLAMS IN THEIR SHELLS, RINSED AND CLEANED OF ANY DIRT OR SAND; DISCARD ANY WITH BROKEN SHELLS

3 LARGE SEA SCALLOPS (ABOUT ¼ POUND), EACH CUT INTO 4 PIECES

1 FRESH PLUM TOMATO, CORED, SEEDED, AND CHOPPED

8 STEMS FRESH ITALIAN FLAT-LEAF PARSLEY, LEAVES ONLY, CHOPPED

SALT AND FRESHLY GROUND BLACK PEPPER

Soak the chickpeas in cold water for 8 hours or longer. Drain and discard the water. Rinse under cold water and drain. Combine the chickpeas with the potato and 8 cups cold water in a large saucepan over medium-high heat. When the water begins to boil, lower the heat and simmer, uncovered, about 1 hour, until the chickpeas are tender. Add the carrot, onion, and celery and cook another 45 minutes. Transfer 2 cups of the chickpea mixture and 1 cup cooking liquid to a food processor. Process until smooth and return to the pot with the rest of the soup.

Meanwhile, heat the olive oil and garlic in a large skillet over medium heat. Add the mussels, clams, and scallops and saute, about 10 minutes, until the mussels and clams open. Discard any shells that remain closed. Take the shellfish from the skillet, remove the mussels and clams from the shells, and coarsely chop. Strain the cooking liquid from the shellfish through a fine-mesh strainer lined with paper towels to filter out any sand and add the liquid to the chickpea soup.

When you are ready to serve, stir the shellfish, tomato, and parsley into the soup and gently heat through, being careful not to boil it. Season with salt and pepper to taste.

MAKES 6 SERVINGS

Merluzzo con lenticchie e pomodori

FRESH COD WITH LENTILS AND TOMATOES

Rino and Lucia Botte are restaurateurs I met years ago in Cremona, where they ran Cerasole, a splendid restaurant. They have since moved to Barile, in the hills of southern Italy, and opened a gracious, charming inn, Locanda del Palazzo, with a spectacular restaurant where Lucia does the cooking. They serve this elegant dish, a new take on a traditional recipe.

5	TABLESPOONS OLIVE OIL
1	SMALL RED ONION, FINELY CHOPPED
1	RIB CELERY, FINELY CHOPPED
1	CLOVE GARLIC, PEELED AND FINELY CHOPPED
1	CUP ITALIAN SMALL BROWN LENTILS OR FRENCH GREEN LENTILS
1	BAY LEAF
	SALT AND FRESHLY GROUND BLACK PEPPER
2	PINTS SMALL CHERRY OR GRAPE TOMATOES, HALVED
2	TABLESPOONS CANOLA OIL
1⅓	POUNDS FRESH COD FILLETS, CUT INTO 4 EQUAL PIECES
2	TABLESPOONS UNBLEACHED WHITE FLOUR
8	STEMS FRESH ITALIAN FLAT-LEAF PARSLEY, LEAVES ONLY, CHOPPED

Heat 2 tablespoons olive oil in a medium saucepan over medium heat. Add the onion, celery, and garlic and cook, stirring, 2 to 3 minutes, until the vegetables begin to soften. Add the lentils, bay leaf, and 4 cups water. Raise the heat to medium-high. When the water begins to boil, lower the heat and simmer, uncovered, about 45 minutes, until the lentils are tender. Season with salt and pepper to taste and cover to keep warm. Discard the bay leaf. Reheat before serving.

Preheat the oven to 450 degrees.

Heat the remaining 3 tablespoons olive oil in a small skillet over medium heat. Add the tomatoes, season with salt and pepper to taste, and saute, stirring occasionally, about 10 minutes, until the tomatoes are soft, the skins have turned orange, and the juices have reduced slightly.

Meanwhile, prepare the fish. Heat the canola oil over medium-high heat in a heavy ovenproof skillet large enough to hold the pieces of fish in one layer without crowding. Lightly dust the fish with the flour, brushing off any excess. Season with salt and pepper. When the oil is hot, add the fish to the skillet and cook, 2 to 3 minutes, until lightly browned. Gently turn the fish over, immediately place the skillet in the oven, and continue cooking, about 7 minutes longer, until the fish flakes easily with a fork. Remove from the oven.

To serve, spoon some of the lentils onto each plate. Place a piece of fish on the lentils and top with some of the cherry tomatoes. Sprinkle each serving with parsley.

Makes 4 servings

STEW OF CANNELLINI AND CLAMS

This is a traditional dish from the regions of Lazio and Campania, in southern Italy. Beans and clams are an inspired combination. The beans take on a marvelous flavor from the lightly spicy clams and garlic. You can use any type of clams, as long as they're very fresh, but you'll have to adjust the quantity of clams depending on the variety. You'll need more East Coast clams with their heavy shells—even the smallest littlenecks—than the smaller, lighter Manila clams from the West Coast. You can prepare the beans in advance and cook the clams just before you plan to serve them. Serve with some good crusty bread so you can soak up the delicious juices.

1	CUP DRIED CANNELLINI OR GREAT NORTHERN BEANS
1	SMALL RED ONION, FINELY CHOPPED
1	RIB CELERY, FINELY CHOPPED
1	SMALL CARROT, FINELY CHOPPED
3	STEMS FRESH THYME
1	STEM FRESH ROSEMARY
	SALT
¼	CUP OLIVE OIL, PLUS MORE FOR SERVING
2	CLOVES GARLIC, PEELED AND FINELY CHOPPED
	PINCH OF PEPERONCINO (RED PEPPER FLAKES)
5	POUNDS SMALL CLAMS, PREFERABLY MANILA CLAMS, RINSED AND CLEANED OF ANY DIRT OR SAND; DISCARD ANY WITH BROKEN SHELLS
15	STEMS FRESH ITALIAN FLAT-LEAF PARSLEY, LEAVES ONLY, CHOPPED

Soak the beans in cold water for 8 hours or longer. Drain and discard the soaking water. Rinse under cold water and drain again. Combine the beans, onion, celery, carrot, thyme, rosemary, and 6 cups cold water in a medium saucepan over medium-high heat. When the water begins to boil, lower the heat and simmer, about 1 hour, until the beans are tender. Discard the herbs. Season with salt and set aside.

Heat the olive oil in a heavy large skillet over medium heat. Add the garlic, peperoncino, and clams and season with salt to taste. Cook, stirring frequently, about 10 minutes, until the clams open. Discard any clams that remain closed. Drain the beans and add them to the clams. Continue cooking, about 5 minutes longer, to heat through. Serve the stew in deep soup bowls with some of the juices from the clams. Add a drizzle of olive oil to each serving and garnish with the chopped parsley.

MAKES 4 SERVINGS

Tonno fresco con fagioli e rucola

SEARED FRESH TUNA WITH WHITE BEANS AND ARUGULA

This recipe is a contemporary adaptation of the traditional canned tuna and white bean dish insalata lessa *(see recipe on page 58)*. It's one of my favorite summer entrees because it's easy and requires a minimum of last-minute cooking, which can be done on an outdoor grill. Fresh wild tuna, the red meat of the sea, is widely available in markets. Be sure the fish is at its freshest—the deep red color and lustrously glossy appearance are usually good signs of freshness—because the steaks are only seared, rather than cooked all the way through, and served very rare. You can prepare the beans well ahead of time.

1	CUP DRIED CANNELLINI, GREAT NORTHERN, OR SORANINI BEANS
1	CLOVE GARLIC, PEELED
2	LARGE LEAVES FRESH SAGE
½	CUP OLIVE OIL
	SALT AND FRESHLY GROUND BLACK PEPPER
2	POUNDS FRESH TUNA STEAK, CUT INTO 4 PIECES
	JUICE OF ½ LEMON
3	OUNCES FRESH ARUGULA, RINSED IN COLD WATER AND DRIED

Soak the beans in cold water for 8 hours or longer. Drain and discard the soaking water. Rinse under cold water and drain again. Combine the beans with the garlic, sage, and 6 cups cold water in a medium saucepan over medium-high heat. When the water begins to boil, lower the heat and simmer, uncovered, about 1 hour, until the beans are tender. Turn off the heat, discard the garlic and sage, and set aside until the beans cool to room temperature. Drain thoroughly and transfer to a serving bowl. Add ¼ cup olive oil, season with salt and pepper to taste, and mix well to combine.

A half hour before you plan to cook the tuna, combine the tuna with the lemon juice, the remaining ¼ cup olive oil, and salt and pepper to taste. Turn to coat both sides of the tuna steaks with the lemon and oil mixture and set aside at room temperature.

Prepare your outdoor grill or preheat a stove-top cast-iron grill over high heat. When the grill is hot, place the tuna steaks on the grill and cook exactly 2 minutes on each side.

Serve immediately, on preheated plates, with beans and arugula on the side.

MAKES 4 SERVINGS

INDEX

P

Conversion Chart

These equivalents have been slightly rounded to make measuring easier.

VOLUME MEASUREMENTS

U.S.	Imperial	Metric
¼ tsp	–	1 ml
½ tsp	–	2 ml
1 tsp	–	5 ml
1 Tbsp	–	15 ml
2 Tbsp (1 oz)	1 fl oz	30 ml
¼ cup (2 oz)	2 fl oz	60 ml
⅓ cup (3 oz)	3 fl oz	80 ml
½ cup (4 oz)	4 fl oz	120 ml
⅔ cup (5 oz)	5 fl oz	160 ml
¾ cup (6 oz)	6 fl oz	180 ml
1 cup (8 oz)	8 fl oz	240 ml

WEIGHT MEASUREMENTS

U.S.	Metric
1 oz	30 g
2 oz	60 g
4 oz (¼ lb)	115 g
5 oz (⅓ lb)	145 g
6 oz	170 g
7 oz	200 g
8 oz (½ lb)	230 g
10 oz	285 g
12 oz (¾ lb)	340 g
14 oz	400 g
16 oz (1 lb)	455 g
2.2 lb	1 kg

LENGTH MEASUREMENTS

U.S.	Metric
¼"	0.6 cm
½"	1.25 cm
1"	2.5 cm
2"	5 cm
4"	11 cm
6"	15 cm
8"	20 cm
10"	25 cm
12" (1')	30 cm

Pan Sizes

U.S.	Metric
8" cake pan	20 × 4 cm sandwich or cake tin
9" cake pan	23 × 3.5 cm sandwich or cake tin
11" × 7" baking pan	28 × 18 cm baking tin
13" × 9" baking pan	32.5 × 23 cm baking tin
15" × 10" baking pan	38 × 25.5 cm baking tin (Swiss roll tin)
1½ qt baking dish	1.5 liter baking dish
2 qt baking dish	2 liter baking dish
2 qt rectangular baking dish	30 × 19 cm baking dish
9" pie plate	22 × 4 or 23 × 4 cm pie plate
7" or 8" springform pan	18 or 20 cm springform or loose-bottom cake tin
9" × 5" loaf pan	23 × 13 cm or 2 lb narrow loaf tin or pâté tin

Temperatures

Fahrenheit	Centigrade	Gas
140°	60°	–
160°	70°	–
180°	80°	–
225°	105°	¼
250°	120°	½
275°	135°	1
300°	150°	2
325°	160°	3
350°	180°	4
375°	190°	5
400°	200°	6
425°	220°	7
450°	230°	8
475°	245°	9
500°	260°	–

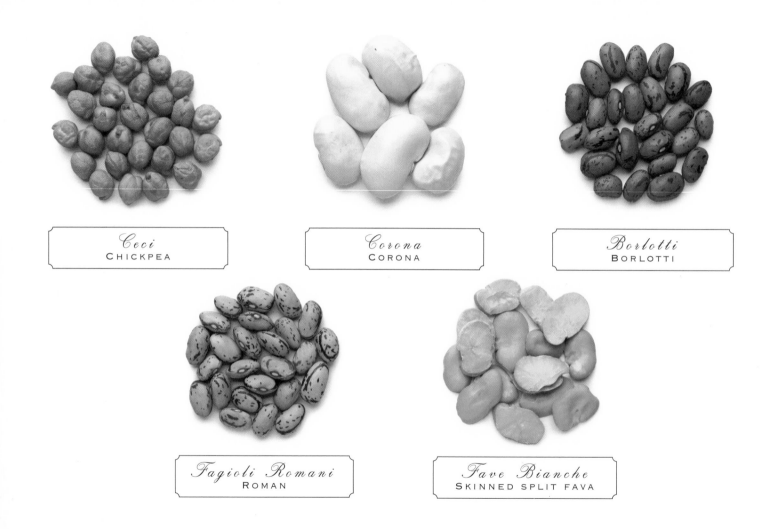

Ceci
CHICKPEA

Corona
CORONA

Borlotti
BORLOTTI

Fagioli Romani
ROMAN

Fave Bianche
SKINNED SPLIT FAVA